Celtic Body Decoration

IMPORTANT NOTE

BODY PAINT IS FOR EXTERNAL USE ONLY

WARNING

Any contact with the eyes should be avoided. However, if you do get paint in the eye, wash your eyes immediately with cold water, or rinse with an eye bath. If symptoms persist then contact your doctor immediately.

THIS IS A CARLTON BOOK

A CIP catalogue record for this book is available from the British Library

ISBN 1 85868 597 4

Project Editor: Lucian Randall
Senior Art Editor: Diane Spender
Copy Editor: Allie Glenny
Editorial Assistant: Heather Dickson
Designer: Andrea Doe
Production: Garry Lewis
Body Painting Consultant: Mark Smith at Screenface, London

Printed and bound in Great Britain

Celtic Body Decoration

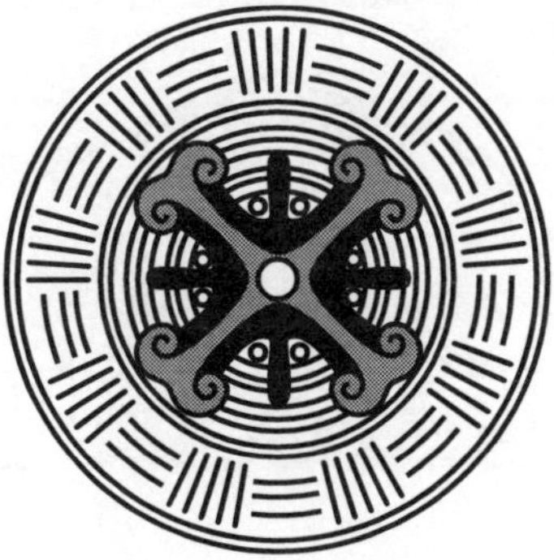

Andy Sloss

CARLTON

contents

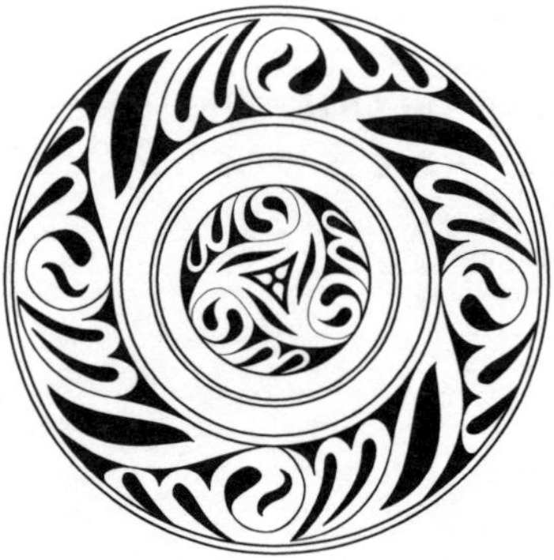

Introduction

Imagine yourself a Roman soldier, highly disciplined, in full battle dress, marching in orderly ranks through a cold, wet land hundreds or thousands of miles from home. Suddenly down from the hills comes a band of demons – some on chariots, some on horseback, most on foot – wearing nothing but swords and shields and covered with disturbing blue images of weird, monstrous animals and disorientating spirals. The Celts' hair, bleached and thick with lime, is plastered to their heads or sticking up like deranged punks'. Above all this a blood-curdling scream rises from every mouth and echoes around the valley, the cacophany growing as the barbarians approach. For the Celts this would have been the best of days, for the Roman foot soldiers probably the worst.

This is one of the overriding pictures we retain today of Celtic culture. The other is of the glorious artwork produced by the Celts after their conversion to Christianity. In Celtic body art the two images meet.

Horrified descriptions by the invading Romans have given rise to the belief that several of the Celtic tribes (such as the Brigantes and the Picts of northern England and Scotland) painted designs on their bodies with blue paint when going into battle. The Celts themselves, however, relied on an oral tradition (their only written records being in the form of funeral inscriptions) and have left no such evidence. Their culture died with them to all intents and purposes. Several books, for example the *Book of the Dun Cow*, contain versions of ancient

Celtic myths, but unfortunately the earliest of these was written in the 9th century, after hundreds of years of Christianization, so they are not totally reliable.

These myths tell us very little about the daily life of the Celtic tribes in Britain, being mainly about heroes and villains. This, together with the fact that no preserved painted bodies have yet been found, means that we have scant direct information about body art. There is, however, a lot that can be deduced from indirect evidence.

Historical references to Celtic body art date from the middle of the 1st century BC, when Caesar (whose histories are famous for being more propaganda than accurate description of the events and peoples) wrote in *Gallic Wars*, 'All the Britons, without exception, paint themselves with woad, which produces a bluish colour.' Later references to the Britons painting themselves can be found in the writings of Pliny, Martial, Mela, Solinus and Herodian in the 3rd century.

The first reference to body art as peculiar to the Picts, however, is only found in the

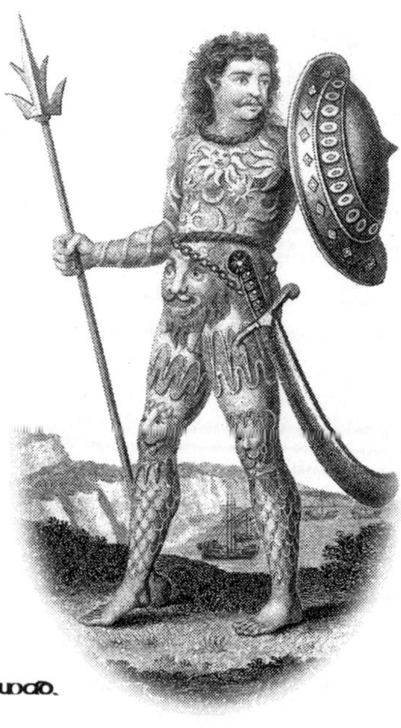

A Victorian fantasy of a British warrior wearing woad.

7th century, in the works of Isidore of Seville. There are several possible reasons for this. It may be that originally all Britons painted themselves but that they gave up their old ways as they became increasingly Romanized, thus leaving the unconquered Picts on the furthest northern fringes of the Roman empire the only remaining users of body paint. The Scots, coming originally from Ireland, may not have had a tradition of body painting; there are no references to it. Alternatively, it is possible that the Picts were always the only body painters but that for effect Caesar described their culture as extending throughout Britain.

In Roman times, and until very recently, many cultural traits of the British Celts pointed to barbarity. The matrilineal descent of Celtic chieftains and the practice of collecting severed heads were bad enough, but going around naked and painting their bodies made them appear even more savage than their continental cousins. From Roman times until the end of the 19th century, expanding empires have agreed that the only way to deal with such savages is to subdue and 'civilize' them.

As for the designs themselves, Herodian recorded that the Celts of northern Britain 'mark their bodies with various figures of all kinds of animals and wear no clothes for fear of concealing these figures'. There is much archaeological evidence that the pre-Christian Celts used an astonishing range of spiral patterns, step patterns and symbols of animals and people (though images of people were much more common in Scandinavia and among the Germanic Celts than in Britain). The spirals and step patterns of the early Celts are well documented; however there is no evidence for the widespread belief that the Celts (like many other 'primitive' cultures) did not make images of living things for spiritual reasons.

Examples of Celtic animal designs survive, for example the Burghead Bull, a stylized image of a bull carved on a stone in Burghead, Inverness. The shape of the hooves and the spiral patterns of the shoulder blades and ear lobes are notable. These features are repeated in most of the great Bibles of northern Britain and Ireland in the evangelists' symbols of lamb and lion. That they appear almost unchanged across such a wide time-span and area indicates that they were popular images with a powerful significance and history in Britain.

The bird, and to a lesser extent dog, images in the Bibles show a similar uniformity. While there are some similarities with German art of the time, their popularity in Britain implies a local tradition dating from long before Christian times. Though there is no solid evidence for this tradition (for even the Pictish symbol stones were carved after the arrival of the Christians) the fact that they appear as fully formed, standardized designs in the manuscripts of the 6th to the 10th century implies that there had been a long period of development. The lack of archaeological evidence for this development indicates that it must have taken place on volatile (i.e. quick to decay) materials. Patterns may have been carved in wood, but it is more likely that they were painted onto wood, stone or the human body, as Caesar and others describe.

Unfortunately, there is no record of who developed and formalized these designs or of what their purpose was. The Celts had always had their Aes Dana (men of arts), but their skills were mainly verbal, and the metal workers who created decorated shields, swords, brooches and mirrors would mainly have been occupied with work of a more mundane variety. However, the arrival of the early Christian monastic settlements changed everything. The first was Candida Casa, founded by St Ninian in Whithorn, south-west Scotland, around 400 AD. Here at last was a structure that would develop the wealth and power necessary to keep a group of people whose primary function was to copy and decorate books. Now artists could dedicate their lives to developing their art – the first uniquely British art form that would influence much later European art.

Evidently vellum and quill pens were a godsend to the Celts. The smooth surface and fine nibs allowed their designs to become smaller and yet more intricate, the detail amazing those who saw them.

It was in borders and decoration that Celtic artists found the scope to show off their skills. Scribes quite quickly dropped as much portraiture and illustration as possible, making decoration the focus of the art. Thus carpet pages were born. These are pages filled to the brim with knotwork, key patterns, interlaced animals, spirals and other traditional Celtic motifs suitable for the hours of contemplation that were the staple diet of the Columban monk.

Centuries earlier the Celts had taken basic fret and step patterns and for some reason rotated the grid. Instead of on the traditional horizontal and vertical, all the setting-out lines were drawn on the diagonal. This dramatically increased the number of possible variations and meant that the edges of the page had to be completely redesigned. So evolved the distinctive Celtic key pattern.

Celtic scribes seem to have adapted the interlace patterns of Roman and Byzantine manuscripts in their work. Whether this was deliberate, or a result of their not understanding the classical method of setting out the originals, does not matter. The change was dramatic. The handful of original possibilities suddenly exploded into an infinite variety of different knots. Despite the rigid geometry at its heart, Celtic knotwork gave scribes the chance really to show their virtuosity. Their books were coveted throughout Europe at the time and are still inspiring us over a millennium later.

The work of the scribes influenced jewellers, blacksmiths and stonemasons, leading to an explosion of creativity and a rapid evolution of styles and skills, all funded by the Church. Where this growth might have eventually led the Celtic artists we will never know, because in 644 AD at the Synod of Whitby the Rome-based Augustine Church outlawed the Celtic Columban Church.

The end was not instant. Pockets of resistance remained (for instance in the Culdees in the remoter areas of northern Britain) for another thousand years. The monasteries' funds began to dry up rather more quickly, and the quality of the artwork declined rapidly. Despite the dispersal of the Columban monks throughout Europe over the next thousand years and the founding of new

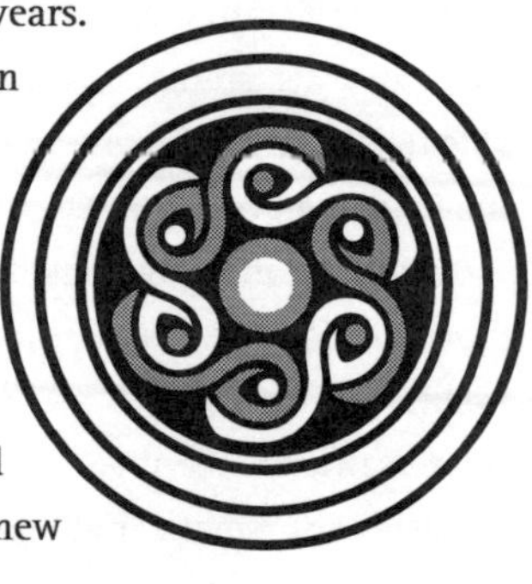

monasteries and scriptoriums based on the Columban system, the golden age of Celtic art was over.

Over the next thousand years Celtic art disappeared, even from countries outside the Christian empire. The Vikings had worked in a similar style for some time, having developed it from the same roots, and continued to design knotwork and interlaced snake and bird images. This style, known as the Urnes style, used much thinner lines than did Celtic art, and a lot of the balance, symmetry and beauty of form were lost.

It was through the 19th-century interest in archaeology and history and the Victorian fashion for decoration that Celtic art was rediscovered. Pioneering work by J. Romilly Allen and George Bain led to the publication of Bain's book Celtic Art: Methods of Construction, in 1951. This started the modern interest both in creating Celtic works of art and in understanding and appreciating them.

By the 1970s Celtic tattoos had started to become popular, first in Britain, then further abroad. At first, while tattooists were getting to grips with the form, almost all the designs were copied from George Bain's book, but as they became more confident in their abilities, they developed new and increasingly complex originals. Nowadays there are tattooists around the world who will make you a unique and fascinating design if you have the patience, nerve and money. Increasingly popular are Celtic designs superimposed on zigzag, lightning-bolt-like lines, drawing inspiration from a wide range of sources – from Maori body art to the works of H.R. Giger. So the Celtic tradition of assimilating and adapting styles from other cultures continues. Now it is your turn to add to the body of Celtic art. Create and enjoy.

Colour

Although this book is in black and white, virtually all Celtic designs were originally coloured. There is even reason to believe that the Celts painted their carved stones, as did the Romans, Greeks and others. The great Bibles were alive with a wide range of colours, the inks and dyes coming from all over Christian Europe and beyond. Items were coloured in a similar way to *champlevé* enamel work. First the outlines were completely drawn in (almost always in black), and then the areas were filled in with flat colours.

It was believed that the Celts used woad, a blue dye, because the both the Romans and the Greeks refer to it repeatedly. However, this idea has been questioned since the discovery of two preserved bodies in a peat bog in Lindow Moss, Cheshire which had copper-based dye on their skins. Unfortunately, the patterns could not be made out. Copper is the basis of verdigris, a green-blue salt known to the Celts. While it is possible that the Celts used verdigris as body paint, it is unlikely, as the Romans knew of the substance, and would probably have recognized it as such. In fact the Romans referred to the Celtic paint as 'vitrum', a word of unknown meaning, but usually translated as 'woad'.

Herodian, in the 3rd century AD, reported: 'They paint their bodies with sundry colours, with all kinds of animals represented in them.' From this statement, and from the Celts' obvious love of colour and skill with it (as can be seen in the great Christian illuminated manuscripts) it seems safe to assume that woad was not the only dye they used. They had knowledge of innumerable vegetable and mineral dyes, and it is very likely that the flamboyant Celt would have used all the colours at his or her disposal to impress or terrify.

The most obvious contender would be madder, a plant which was then and is now used to create an extremely wide range of colours; from warm red to deep blue. The Celts were reportedly able to dye cloth in any shade of purple (purple dye being a very important and expensive commodity to the Romans). There are also references to Celts using blackberry juice as a dye. Their knowledge and skills must have gone much further. It is reasonable to assume that the Celts had a full palette of colours for their body art and that they used it.

Although a wide variety of colours was available to the Celtic scribe, even the most complex knotwork border never contains more than four. One of the colours is used as a

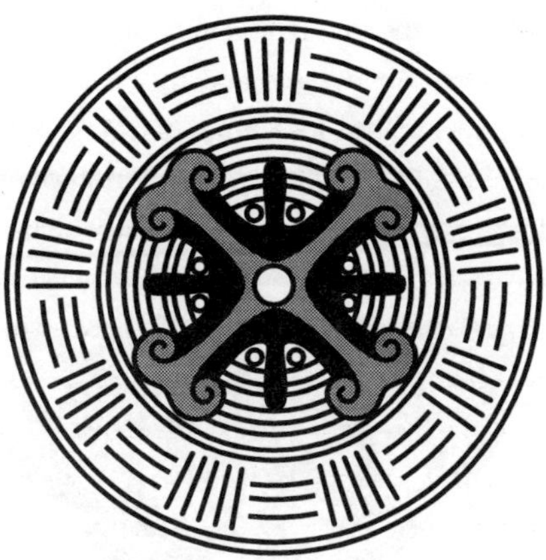

contrasting background. Scribes could put a small range of colours to exceptional effect, as in the Lichfield Gospels. They used strong contrasts when possible, so that from a distance where detail was lost, the colours made a pattern of their own. Often this was achieved simply by setting light and dark against each other. This practice probably originates in the metalwork of the mirror backs found in Britain, in which the spirals have alternating areas of crosshatch and plain metal. The eye jumps from one image to the other, each of which has its own symmetry well as balancing with one another.

By the time of the great Bibles, experience in the use of colour had refined this style. A favourite colour combination was green, red and yellow, because green and red, being opposite colours, stand out from each other, while yellow, being so much lighter and brighter, jumps out from both. For this reason yellow tended to be used sparingly as a highlight, filling far less area than the other two colours. The Celts knew many tricks like this for making their designs vivid while maintaining a harmony between the colours.

When choosing the range of colours for your work it is best to make copies of the designs and try different combinations of colours on them. Then look at them from a distance and see which looks best. With practice you will develop an eye for which colour combinations work best for which designs.

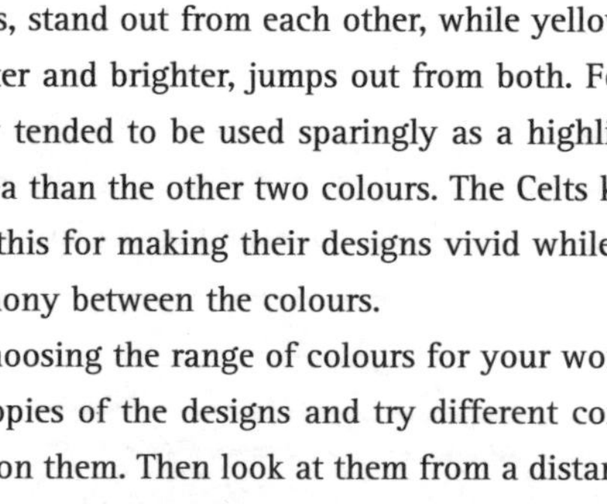

the Picts

The Picts, or 'painted people', were one of the last tribes of the great Celtic culture, and their story is a shadowy one. The first mention of the Celts is by the Greeks, who say that they lived along the coast of the Atlantic and the North Sea. By the time of Ephorus, in the 4th century BC, they were numerous and united enough to be named as one of the four great barbarian peoples in the world. This unity was not, as far as is known, that of a nation or empire, but more cultural in nature.

The name 'picti' first appeared in 297 AD in a reference to enemies of Roman Britain. This was around the time that the two large tribes of the area, the Caledonii and the Maeatae, joined together to become the Picts. From then until their numbers dwindled in the 9th century AD, they are mentioned often, along with the Scots and the Saxons. In fact it was in order to fight off the Picts that the Saxons were invited to Britain from mainland Europe, only to turn on their allies, take over most of England and form the basis of English culture. Meanwhile, the Vikings took over the Pictish lands of the north, and the south of Pictland was combined with Dalraida in the west to form Scotland.

Most of the artwork in the majority of books on the subject comes from the last centuries of Celtic art, when the Christian church created its glorious illuminated manuscripts and metalwork. These intricate designs, combining formal geometry with the most complex of freehand patterns, are what Celtic art is best known for. It seems that the meeting of two completely different styles – the formalism of Byzantine, Greek and Roman sources and the free-flowing curves of the Celts – produced a short burst of incredible creativity among the Picts and their neighbours in Northumbria and Ireland. Herodian wrote, 'They paint their bodies with sundry colours, with all kinds of animals represented in them'; it is likely that most of the designs used by the Picts were the traditional pre-Christian motifs of true Celtic art.

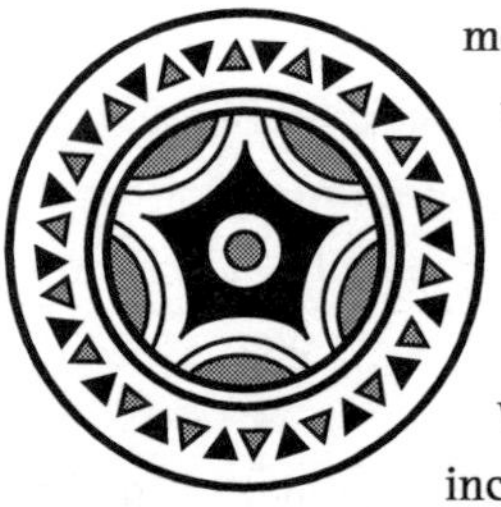

Almost all developments in Celtic art occurred in times of increase in wealth. Invasion and trade led to an increase in the number of decorated objects produced. Trade also brought in new artistic sources of inspiration, thus giving rise to a wider variety of designs used in decoration in each phase of expansion and growth.

Let's now take a step back and look at the history that would ultimately give birth to the Pictish culture. By 800 BC, the beginning of what is known as the Halstatt culture, the characteristics that we associate with Celtic art had been developed. Animal designs (zoomorphs), elegant curves, rich spiral-based design, knotwork and fretwork were all in evidence. These motifs appear to have evolved from the pieces that were imported from the south and east. As they were to show time and again over the centuries, the Celts were no mere copiers, but used whatever influences were to hand to develop their own unique style.

Halstatt art rapidly developed as the Celts became richer through expansion and trade. Around 550 BC, for instance, a German chief was buried in a silk cloak that is presumed to have come originally from China.

Next came the La Tène culture, lasting approximately from 500 BC to 100 AD (the dates vary around Europe, with developments in skills, technology and art styles tending to arrive later in the north and west). The period is named after a spot where a large number of items were found in Lake Neuchâtel. It is assumed that this was a site for votive offerings.

Offerings in water (wells, pools, lakes, streams and rivers) seem to span the entire history of Celtic culture. There are still places today in Britain and Ireland where springs are decorated, though usually with religious symbols rather than with swords and shields. The weapons that have come down to us tend to be unused, and have usually been found in water, where they would have been thrown as offerings to the gods for peace and prosperity. Indeed, a large proportion of all items recovered were originally such votive offerings. Perhaps we can presume that the weapons were not needed in a time of relative peace.

But this peace was destined to end. Between about 100 BC and 100 AD the La Tène culture was almost wiped out by the growing Roman empire. Only the north-western coast of Europe held out, retaining much of its culture and absorbing only what it wanted, which is why the final flowering of Celtic art took place in the British Isles.

This then is the culture that the Picts evolved from and which they continued to develop, using art forms in new and fascinating ways. The remaining 200 or so carved standing stones (a fraction of the number that originally decorated the landscape) show a wealth of creativity, ranging from enigmatic symbol stones to ornate crosses. While the artwork of the crosses, as of the illuminated manuscripts, has been studied and argued over for centuries by art historians, the symbol stones have been ignored to a large extent, because there is nothing like them in the rest of Europe, and thus their history is untraceable.

It is almost certain that the symbols on the stones were used as body art by the Picts, but the question remains: what were they for? Various explanations have been put forward over the years, the most probable being that they were tribal or clan symbols, like the later tartans of the Scots. It is unlikely that they were used as shamans use animal symbols (to take on an animal's characteristics) as they are so often found on the Christian slab stones. Neither is it plausible that they were merely decorative, as the images would then vary from artist to artist, and these symbols are highly formalized.

As these symbols are described as being used by warriors in battle, it may be that they were used as a form of anti-camouflage. Camouflage is useless in hand-to-hand combat, but in a world with little colour, weird, eye-catching designs in brilliant contrasting colours might help to distract your opponent just enough to give you the edge. When fighting for your life was the norm, any help would be welcome.

Finally, nationalists and rebels, such as William Wallace, would have used body art as a way of implying a historical legitimacy to their cause.

Whatever its function, we can now appreciate the art of the Picts for its enigmatic beauty and unfathomable power.

Creating Your Own Celtic Body Art

This section is about body painting techniques and materials which are commercially available. The traditional dyes used by the Celts, such as woad and madder, are not discussed here because they are hard to find and still harder to use. In the main we will be talking about body paint, which is temporary and can be cleaned off, rather than dyes, which stain the skin and so last much longer. Theatrical make-up, such as cake, is not covered because it is difficult to apply and remove, and easy to smudge. If you are painting these designs for theatrical or film use, you should consult a theatrical make-up manual.

There are all sorts of ways to use these designs, from small images on ankles, shoulders and arms, through painted armbands, waistbands and torcs, to full body decoration as described by historians. Experiment – after all, you can wash it off if you don't like it.

Safety First

All the techniques and materials listed below are designed to be safely applied to the skin, but every person is different, and you may develop an allergic reaction to some paints or dyes.

Before trying new paints on yourself or anyone else, always test for a reaction by applying a small amount of paint to the inside of the elbow. Leave this for an hour or so. If there is no reaction (and there almost never will be), it should be safe to cover larger areas with paint.

Materials

Brushes

For these designs it is best to have four brushes:

- one thin round brush for fine detail and touching up any smudged areas,
- one medium round brush for outlines,
- one medium flat brush for filling in areas and for painting lines that vary in width (for a pen-like line) and
- one large round brush for filling in large areas of colour.

All brushes should be as soft as possible so as not to irritate the skin. Soft brushes also hold paint better, make smoother and more even lines, and are easier to clean. Sable and squirrel (artificial) are the best. After use brushes should be cleaned in warm soapy water (do not use detergent), and kept in a jar with the bristles upwards so that they do not bend.

Face Paints

The obvious choice is water-soluble face paint because it is relatively cheap and, being designed for painting onto children, is non-toxic. These paints are available from large toy shops and department stores, and come in small palettes or individual pots. They are easy to apply and dry quickly. Some brands smudge more easily than others (depending on the amount of grease in the paints) so it is worth experimenting.

Face paints come in range of bright colours which are very suitable for Celtic designs, and are opaque. Body paints can also be used for body art. Being water based and non-toxic they are completely safe, quick drying and easy to use. Liquid body paints are the most suitable, with Fardel offering a range of over 150 colours. For fine detail or larger surface areas, these paints are suited to both brush painting and airbrushing.

Textile Acrylics

These are designed for airbrushing onto cloth, but they work well on skin and are non-toxic. They dry quickly and don't rub off easily, and because they are made for textiles they are not as prone to cracking and peeling as ordinary acrylics. Nevertheless, they wash off easily in soap and water. Though intended for airbrushing, they work with ordinary brushes.

Airbrush Make-up

This is safer and more flexible than fabric acrylics, but also more expensive. It is made by Kryolan, and the range is called Starmist. Airbrush make-up is really only worth buying if you want to cover a lot of the body quickly or are working for a commercial client, for instance on a photo shoot. Airbrushing is useful for smooth shading, especially over large areas or when using stencils.

For a realistic and opaque tattoo look, it is worth investing in temporary tattoo ink. Before you commence, clean the skin with alcohol. Dip the brush into the ink, brush it against the side of the bottle, then paint as desired. Use either free-hand designs or follow the waxed paper technique to transfer the design to the skin. You can then fill in the gaps with the selected colour ink. Ink is available in many colours and major ranges are produced by Temptu and Urban Decay. Set the ink with a light dusting of baby powder. The design should last three to five days. Remove using cotton wool soaked in baby oil or alcohol.

Cleaning Up

Cold cream and cosmetic cleansers are best for removing water-based and oil-based paints. Baby wipes are also very effective for removing water-based paints.

Smooth a layer of cold cream over the design, leave it for a minute and then gently rub it off with cotton wool balls or soft tissues. If necessary, repeat until all the paint has gone. Patience does the job much better than brute force.

If you get water-based paint on your clothes, wash it out with cold water followed by detergent. If the paint is oil-based, the detergent should be used first.

techniques

Fake Tattoos

This technique can be used to transfer complicated designs to the skin. These can then be filled in with any type of body paint. Using a dark blue or black ball-point pen, copy your design (in reverse if you want it a particular way round) onto the smoothest, shiniest paper you can find. Waxed paper is the best, as you can trace the design through it (though ball-point pens tend not to work so well on waxed paper). Place the design face down on the body and rub it from behind with cotton wool dipped in acetone (nail polish remover). This will make the ink transfer to the skin. If the ball-point pen does not work on your chosen paper, try a felt-tip pen, but the image will be much fainter and less sharp.

With the outline marked, you can now fill in the areas with colour. For a temporary tattoo it is best to use children's felt-tip pens. They are designed to be (accidentally) applied to the skin and so are safe and easy to remove. Being translucent, they do not obscure the surface of the skin like paints but let it show through as do real tattoos. For filling in, the broader the pen nib the better. Chisel-tipped pens are handy, as they can be used for fine lines as well as filling. As these inks are water-soluble, they should only be used where there will be no water or sweat.

Recently Halawa Henna Products have brought out a range of coloured henna powders. These can be used to produce semi-permanent designs like the Indian bindi markings.

Painting

Having chosen your design and drawn it to the scale you want, trace it onto a piece of waxed paper using a thin, dark felt-tip pen. The lines will be patchy but good enough to use as a guide. Another method is to lie the sheet with your design on top of something soft (for example, a piece of cotton or several sheets of scrap paper) and prick holes with a pin along the lines. Place it on the skin and rub the design with a sponge dipped in paint giving you a dotted outline to follow.

The second step is to fill in the areas with the colours of your choice, painting up to the marked outline. Remember to rinse the brushes in clean, warm water between colours or they will become 'muddy'. To avoid smudging parts that are already painted, do not rest your hand on the skin when painting. Practise steadying your hand with the tip of the little finger, using the lightest pressure possible.

Next paint in the outline in a darker colour. Try to draw lines in one smooth stroke rather than using a lot of short strokes, as this gives a much smoother, more fluid line. The centre of the line should follow the edge of the area that you previously painted so that half is on paint and half on skin. The outline is left until last so that it is of an even width throughout.

If you are painting knotwork, you can use a common technique of the Celts by putting a lighter (usually yellow) central line down the middle of the filled area. This should be done after the outline is complete in order to centre the line as accurately as possible. Another decorative finish that is often seen in Celtic manuscripts is 'rubrification', which consists of putting small red dots all around the outline. These should be added after the outline is complete. Traditionally this was the order in which scribes worked when illuminating the great Celtic Bibles.

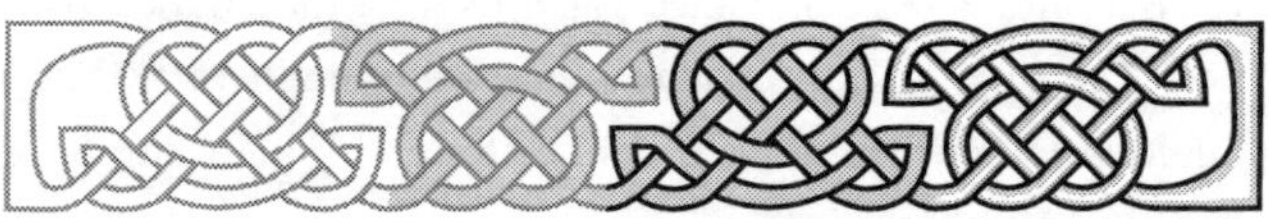

Stencilling

Stencilling is suitable for covering large areas with a repeated pattern or for painting the same design on several people. It allows you to create subtle shading – unlike the Celts, who always used flat colours. Key patterns are particularly suited to stencilling, as you can maintain an even width more easily when cutting a stencil than when painting, and when airbrushed in several colours they look very impressive. When using stencils, more time is spent on preparation and less on the application of paint – which again is useful when applying the same design repeatedly.

The simplest way to make a stencil is to draw your pattern to the size and colour you want it to be on the body. Trace the outline onto tracing paper or photocopy it onto copy paper. Using low-tack spray adhesive, stick it onto stencil paper (available from art and craft shops). You can make your own stencil paper by rubbing both sides of a sheet of card with cotton wool dipped in oil to make it waterproof. Use as little oil as possible to give an even covering.

Referring to the coloured version, cut a stencil for each colour. Lay the copy on the first stencil and cut out the pieces of the design that are to be painted one colour, cutting through both the copy and the stencil. Unpeel the copy from the first stencil and stick it to a second and repeat for the second colour and so on for each of the colours.

Again using low-tack spray adhesive on the stencil, stick it to the body and airbrush the paint on. The small airbrushes available from model shops are perfect for the job as long as you choose a model with replaceable paint jars. These make changing the colour very easy: you simply unscrew the jar of paint, spray some clean water through the airbrush and insert a different coloured paint jar.

Repeat with each of your stencils, taking care to align the different colours. When you have finished you can add an outline, or any other decoration you want, with a brush.

Early Celtic Art

These designs come from the La Tène period and show that the Celts' love of geometry was established long before the Christians brought their influences. Despite the fact that they are made of circles, spirals and freehand curves, almost every one of these designs contains an element of symmetry. Usually the design is reflected in one or two planes (indicated with dotted lines), and occasionally, as in the case of the spiral border, they are rotated.

This style was used to decorate all sorts of objects, from the most ornate shields to the most mundane pottery, so it is more than likely that the body artists of the time used the same motifs for their art. These are just a handful of the thousands of designs and variations that the Celts used in their long history, but they will give you a background from which to develop your own style and designs.

These images, not often seen in books of Celtic art, are included here for two reasons: firstly, they are the most likely style of the Celtic body artist; secondly, they allow you to develop an 'eye' for Celtic art and to practise the basics before moving on to the later, more complex forms of the Christian period – much as the Celts themselves did.

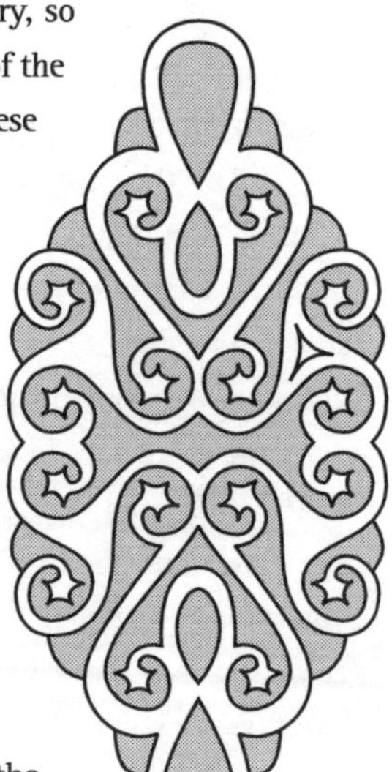

Plaque: Waldasgeheim, Germany

You can use circular objects to mark out the lines. Bottles and jars, and their lids and tops come in a range of sizes and can be used in either of two ways: firstly, by pressing the object against the skin you make an impression that can be traced over before it fades. Secondly, you dip the neck of the bottle or jar in the body paint or dye and then apply it to the skin. With this method the line is often uneven and needs tidying up.

All these designs were used as repeat borders around a flagon from Waldasgeheim in Germany. They are typical of the circle-based designs of Germany up to around the 4th century BC. The style was becoming freer at this time, and it is sometimes easy to see animals 'hidden' in the designs of this and later centuries.

plaque/brooch: kleinaspergle, germany

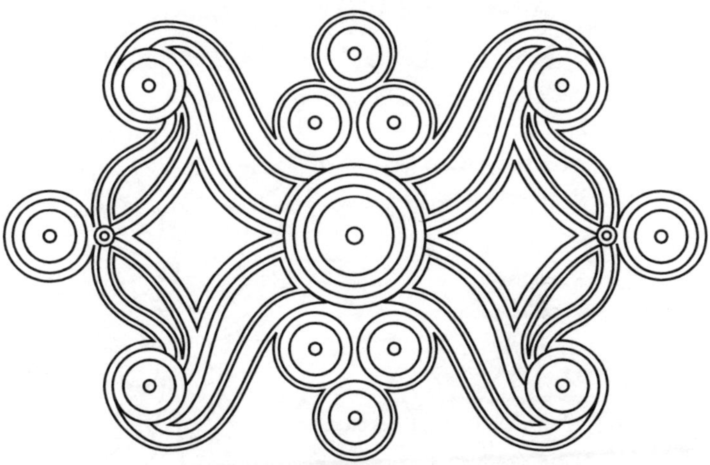

scabbard: wetwang, england

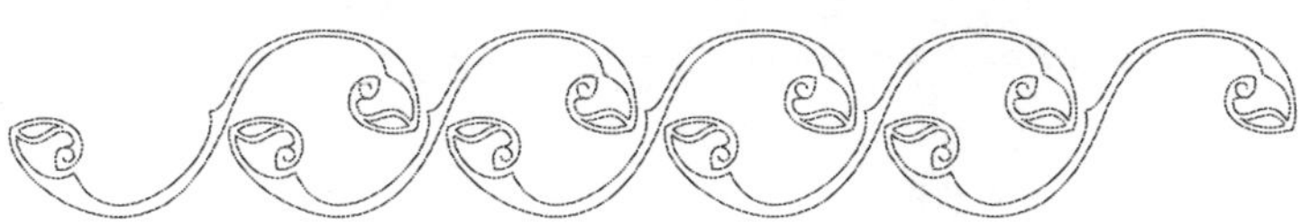

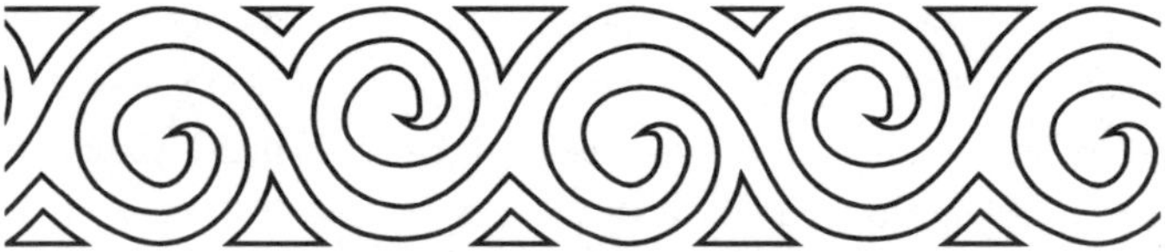

Torc: Jonchery-sur-Suippes, France

Ring: Rodenbach, Germany

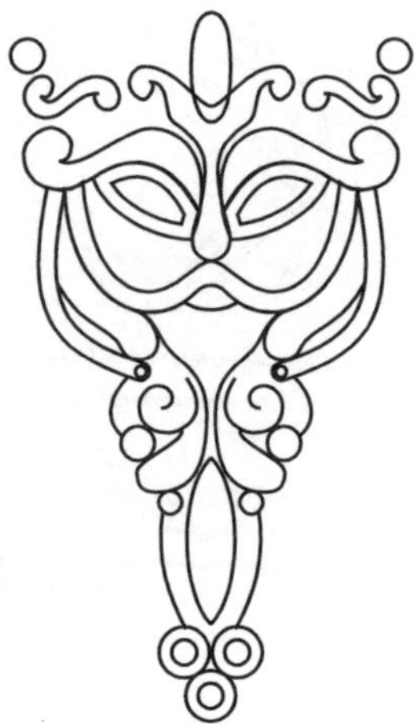

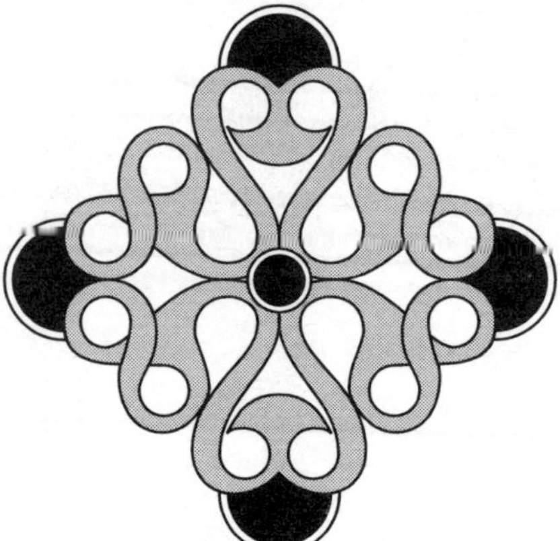

Plaque: Waldasgeheim, Germany

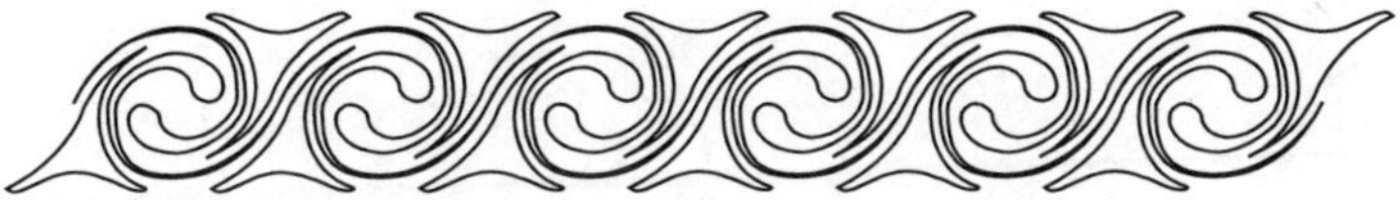

Pottery: Champagne, France

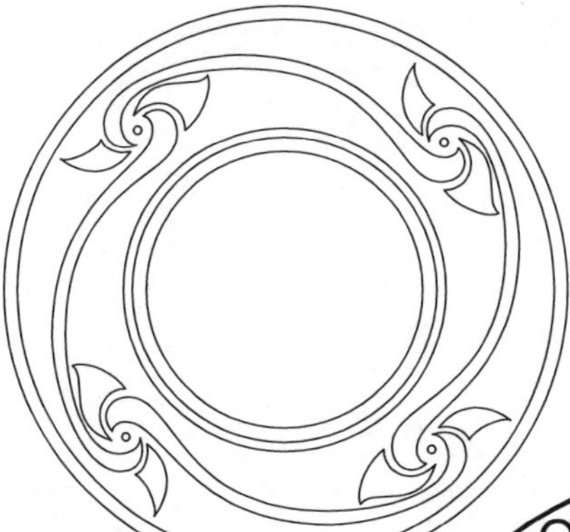

Shield boss:
Polden Hills, England

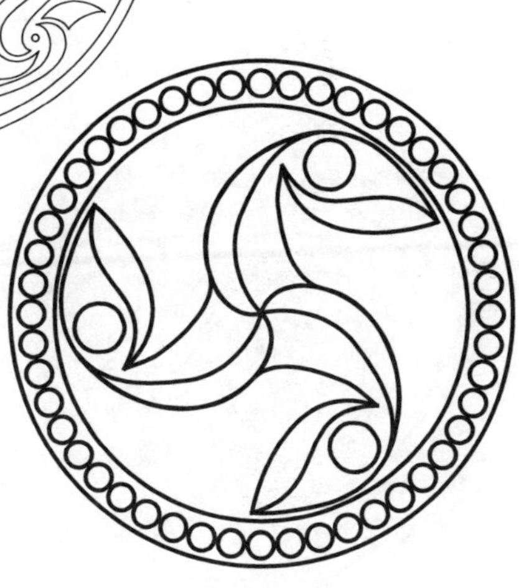

Linch pin: Kirkburn,
England

Scabard: Toome, Ireland

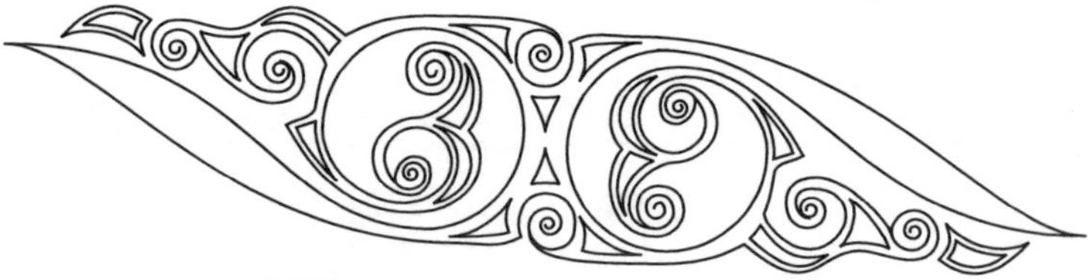

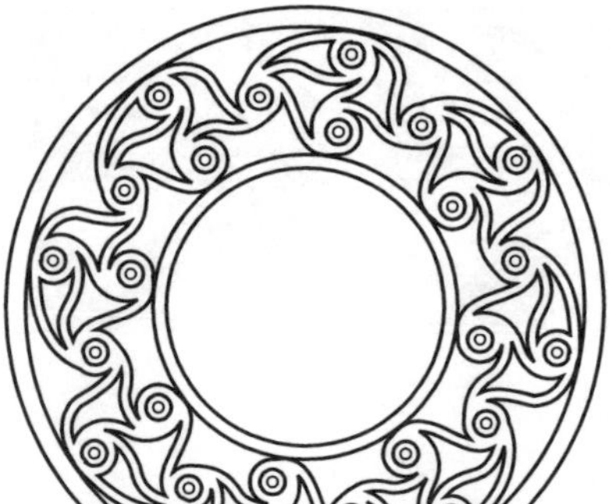

Drinking horn:

Schwarzenbach, Germany

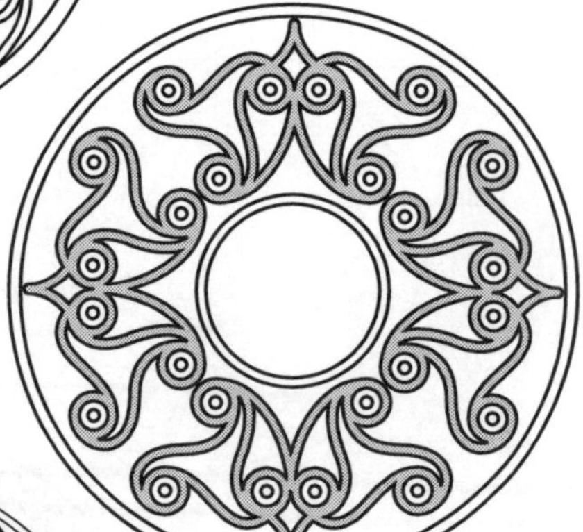

Base of bowl:

Schwarzenbach, Germany

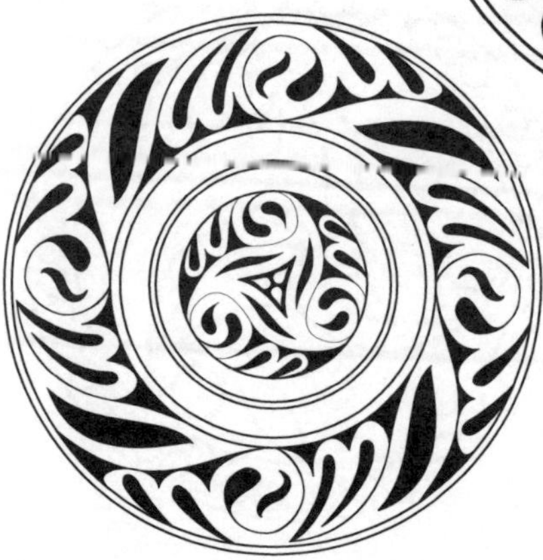

Bowl:

Saulces-Champenoises, France

Mirrors

Mirrors were very popular among the Celts, who valued cleanliness and appearance rather more than many of their 'civilized' contemporaries. They are often found at bronze age archaeological sites and burials, so it is likely that every person of any wealth or position had their own and that it was a valued personal possession. They have been assumed to be associated with women, but there is no archaeological basis for this assumption. The sexual bias is more likely to be a modern one.

The shape of these mirrors is always the same. The mirror itself is in the shape of a lily pad, with a handle made of flattened rings and a loop at the bottom (presumably to hang it up). Often the mirror and its handle are attached by an ornamented joint in the shape of an animal's head, as if it were biting the mirror. In the following examples the lily-pad shape has been simplified into a circle to make it more appropriate to use in body art.

The designs on the back of these mirrors show the greatest variety and intricacy of pre-Christian spiral art. They are, almost without exception, reflected in the vertical plane in line with the axis of the handle, but no two are ever the same.

It is this individuality, along with this object's frequent occurrence, that implies that to the Celt a mirror was a highly personal item. It is not hard to imagine some kind of rite of passage in which the Celt earned his or her own mirror, and with it a stronger sense of self.

La Tène mirrors have no enamel or other colour on them, but are divided into dark and light areas. The light areas would have been polished and the dark areas filled with crosshatching. This is a useful technique when using only one colour. In fact, much of the beauty of the sinuous curves is lost when filled with solid colour; a partial filling allows the eye to jump between the light and dark designs as in an optical illusion. When creating your own designs, pay close attention to the balance between the light and dark areas, as therein lies the beauty.

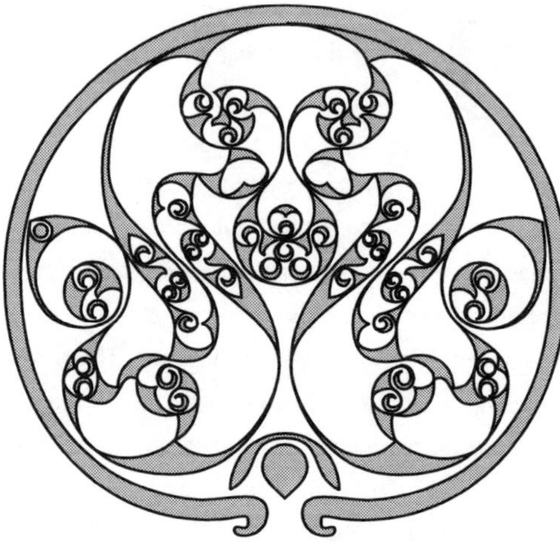

Desborough, England

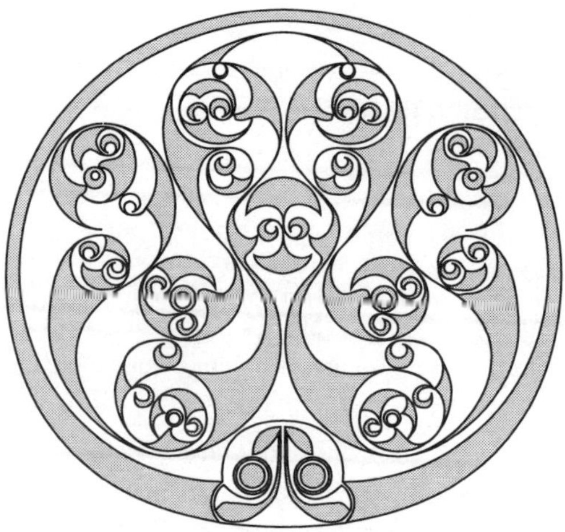

Holcombe, England

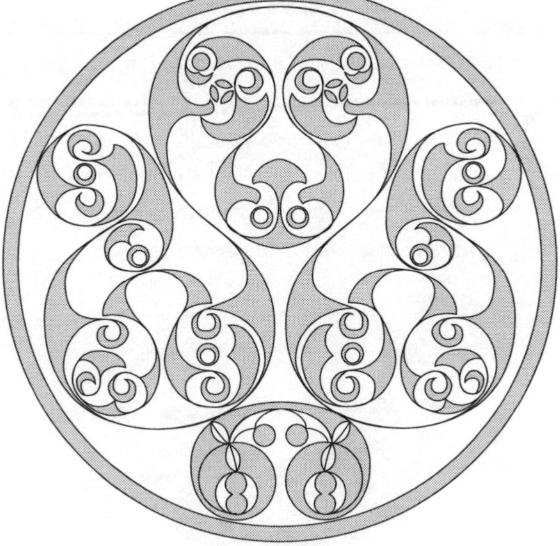

Birdlip, England

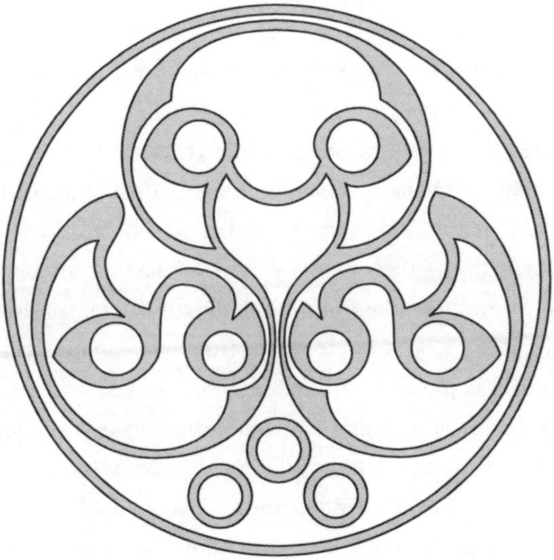

Holcombe, England

torcs

Possibly the best known item of jewellery worn by the Celts was the torc, a large gold or bronze necklace. It is said that in battle a torc was all the Celt wore, other than war paint. They were almost always penannular (almost a ring, with a round 'boss' at each end).

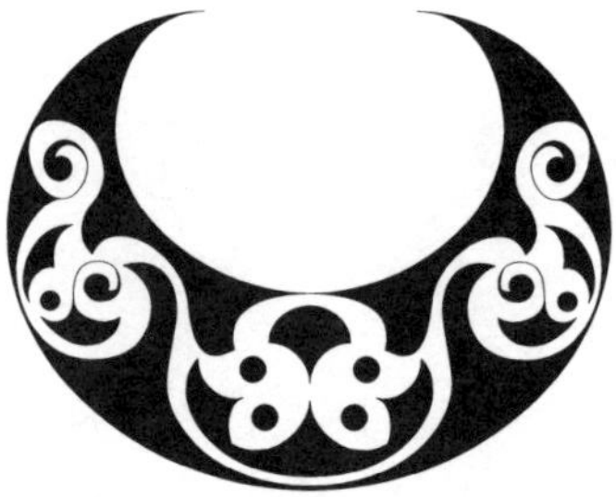

Auchendolly Scotland

These bosses were sometimes separate, sometimes interlocking and sometimes connected by a chain. Often torcs were made up simply of multiple twisted strands of gold melted together at the ends, though a few had designs carved or moulded into them, and some of the later ones had coloured enamel champlevé designs. Most of the early designs were bands of interlocking spirals, all slightly different variations on a basic spiral shape. Otherwise they were almost invariably reflected across the vertical line (the front of the throat) like mirror designs.

These designs are not from torcs but from strap hoops, because torcs were designed as pieces in 3D and would not work when painted on skin. Strap hoops of a similar date and shape make a suitable substitute. When body painting, torcs are a good image to start with, as they were worn by all Celtic warriors, are relatively simple in design, and once painted onto the body do not require you to be naked to show off your artwork.

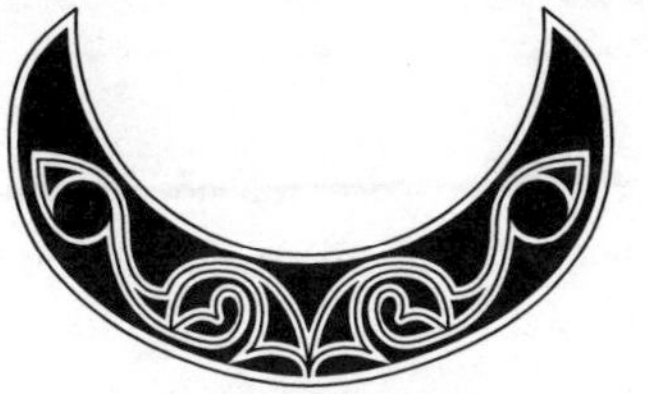

Lakenheath, England

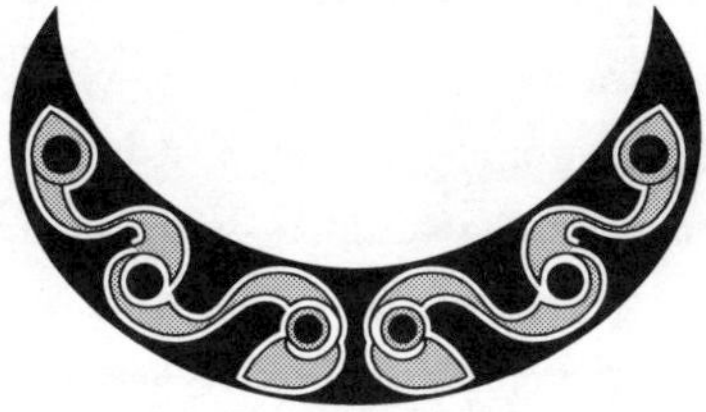

Bolton, England

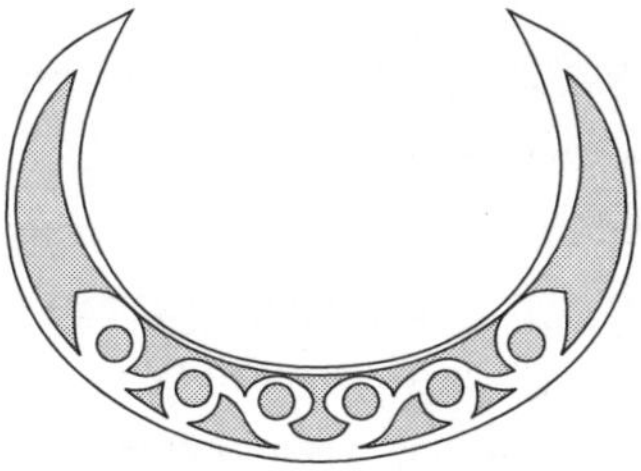

Colchester, England

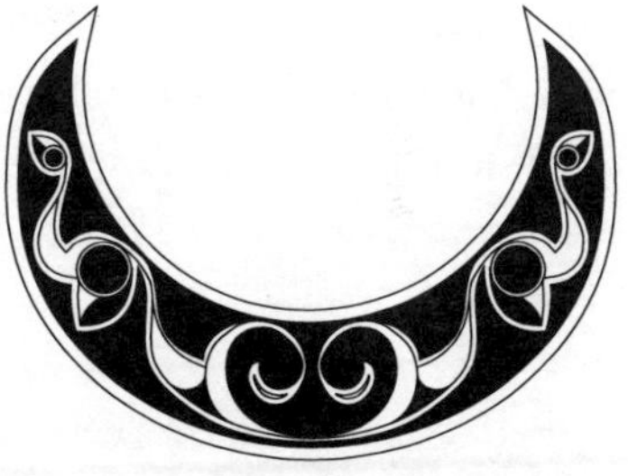

Westhall, England

Colchester, England

Spirals

While knotwork is what we now see as typical of Celtic art, the true signature of the traditional (ie: pre-Christian) form is in fact the spiral. There are spirals in one form or another on almost every pre-Christian decorated object, from standing stones to the most ornate jewellery. The spirals used were rarely the simple single or double line spirals that we see today. As in all aspects of their art, the Celts improvized and developed from the basics to create an entirely new vocabulary of designs.

Names like 'trumpet spiral' and 'duck's head' have been give to the common shapes that make up these spirals, but it is not important to know these names. A wide range of examples is given here for you to practise with. Once you have mastered these, it should be fairly simple to combine different elements to form your own unique spiral designs.

In this section we begin to move into the Christian era of Celtic art. A few of the more basic spiral designs are from the bronze and iron ages, but to an extent these have already been covered in the Mirror and Torc section. The spirals in the illuminated manuscripts, like the rest of the artwork, tend to be much more elaborate, and as such should not be attempted until you are used to drawing the earlier, simpler designs.

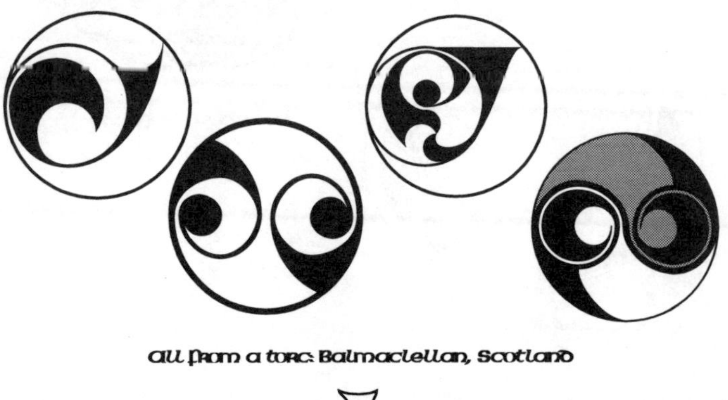

All from a torc: Balmaclellan, Scotland

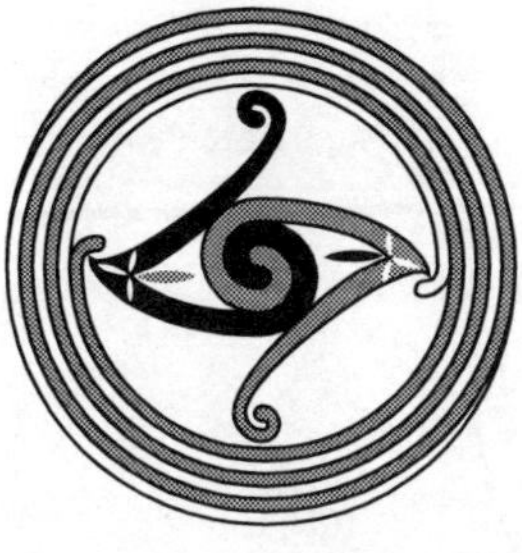

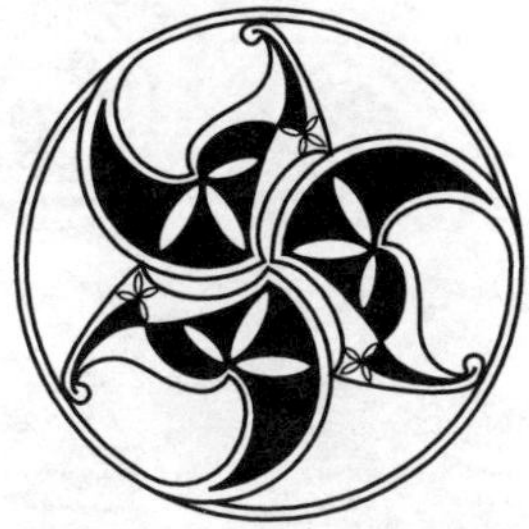

Variations on the three spiral patterns below can be seen throughout the later Celtic period. This is because of their basic geometry. A circle can fit seven smaller ones, each a third of the diameter of the large circle, perfectly inside itself, as in the two designs on the left. The spiral on the right is made up of a large circle, two spirals based on circles half its size and two spirals based on circles as large as will fit in the remaining space. By rotating half of the design the work is made even easier.

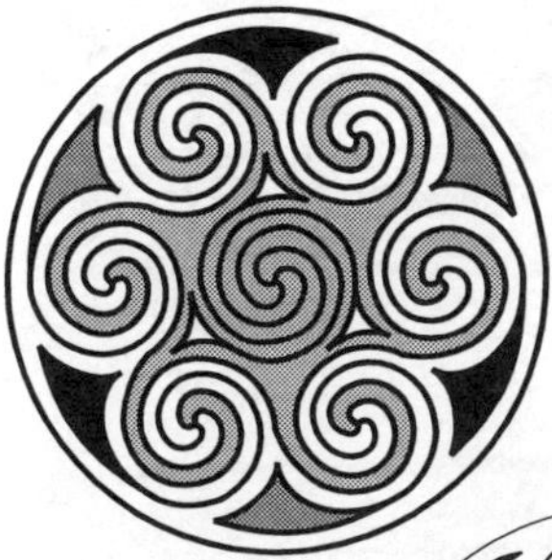

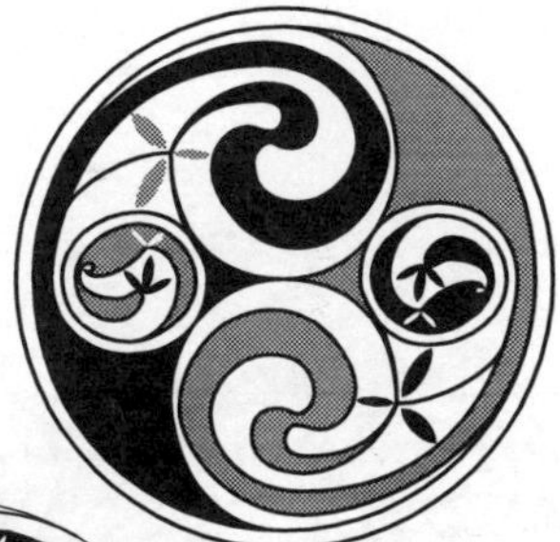

Aberlemno Stone (and others): Scotland

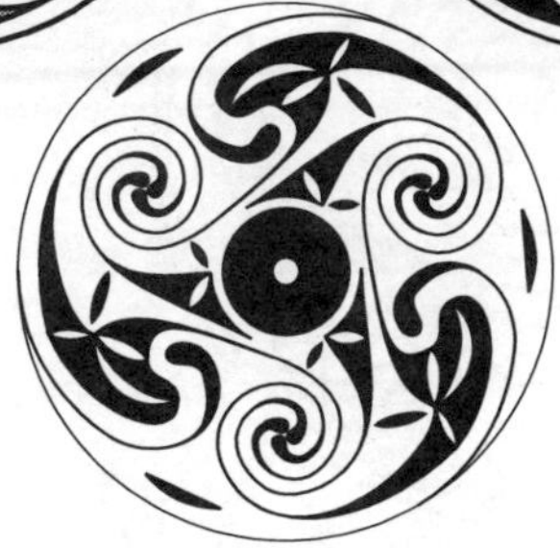

Book of Lindisfarne

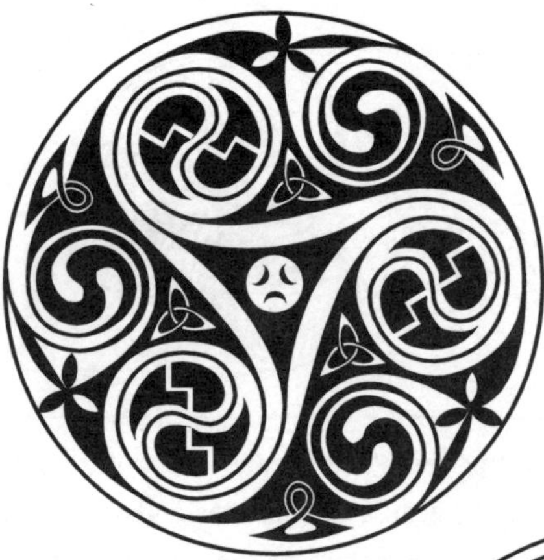

Book of kells

Book of Durrow

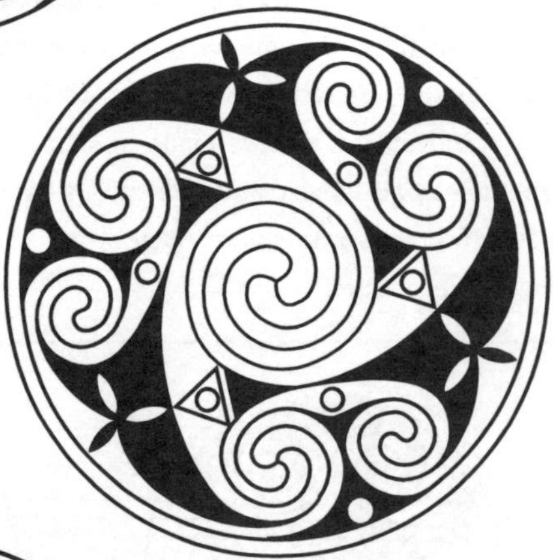

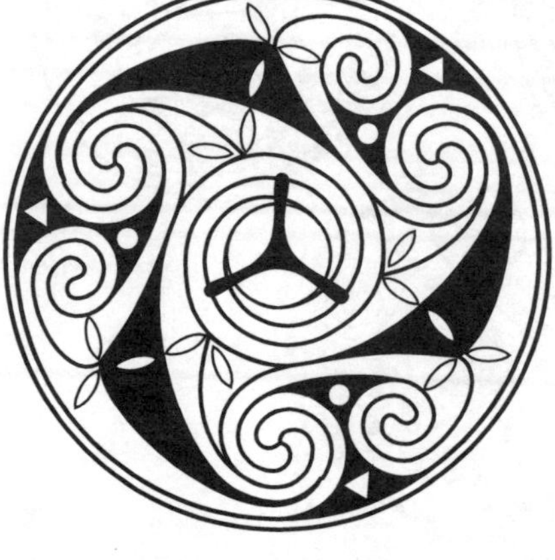

Book of Durrow

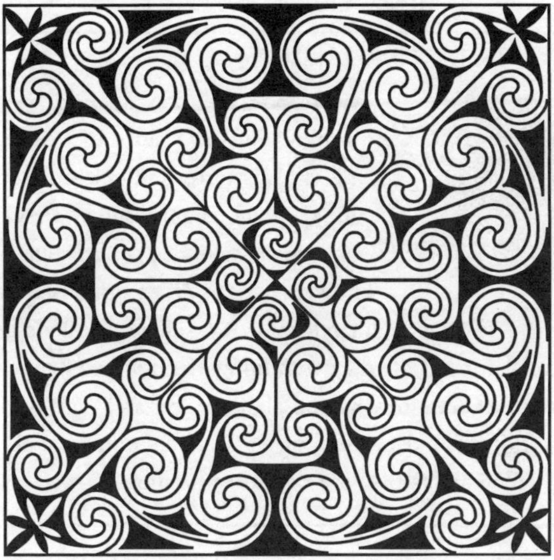

Shandwick Stone, Scotland

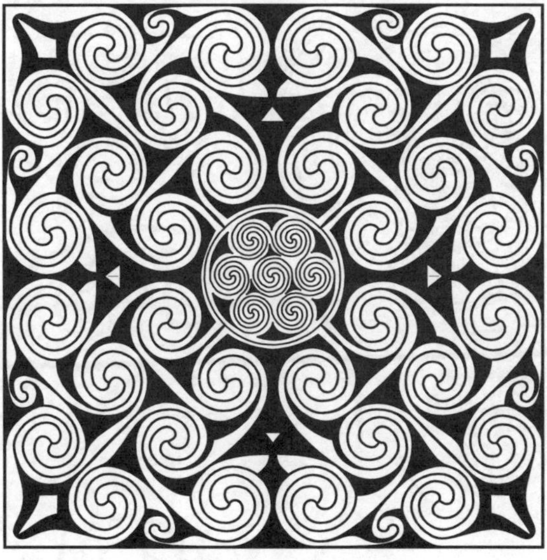

Cadboll Stone, Scotland

Circle Designs

Circle designs, like spirals, are found throughout the history of Celtic art from the early swords and shield bosses to the final great manuscripts. They do not appear to have had a particular meaning, but were used to fill an otherwise empty circular space. They tend, therefore, to be simple spiral or geometric shapes rotated to fill the area with little attention being paid to them. The number of rotations has no significance, as it can be anything from two to twelve, depending on the design. Four, six and eight are the most common, as they are the easiest to draw.

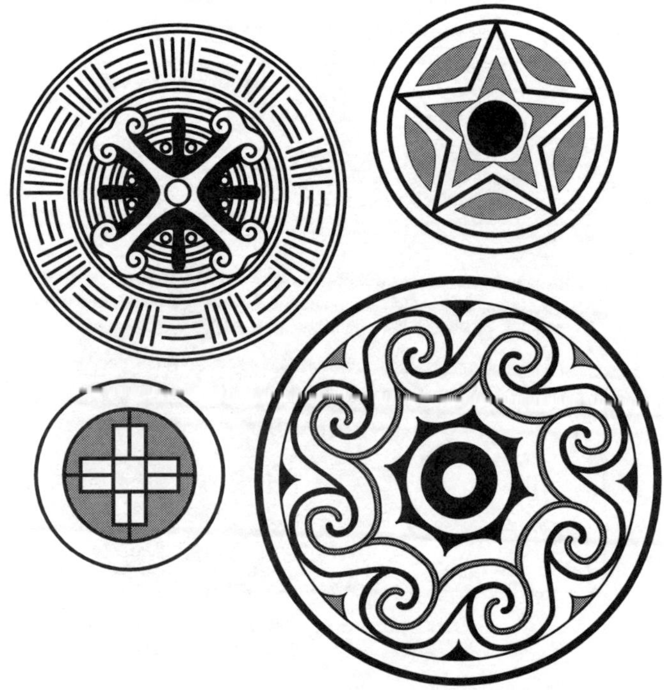

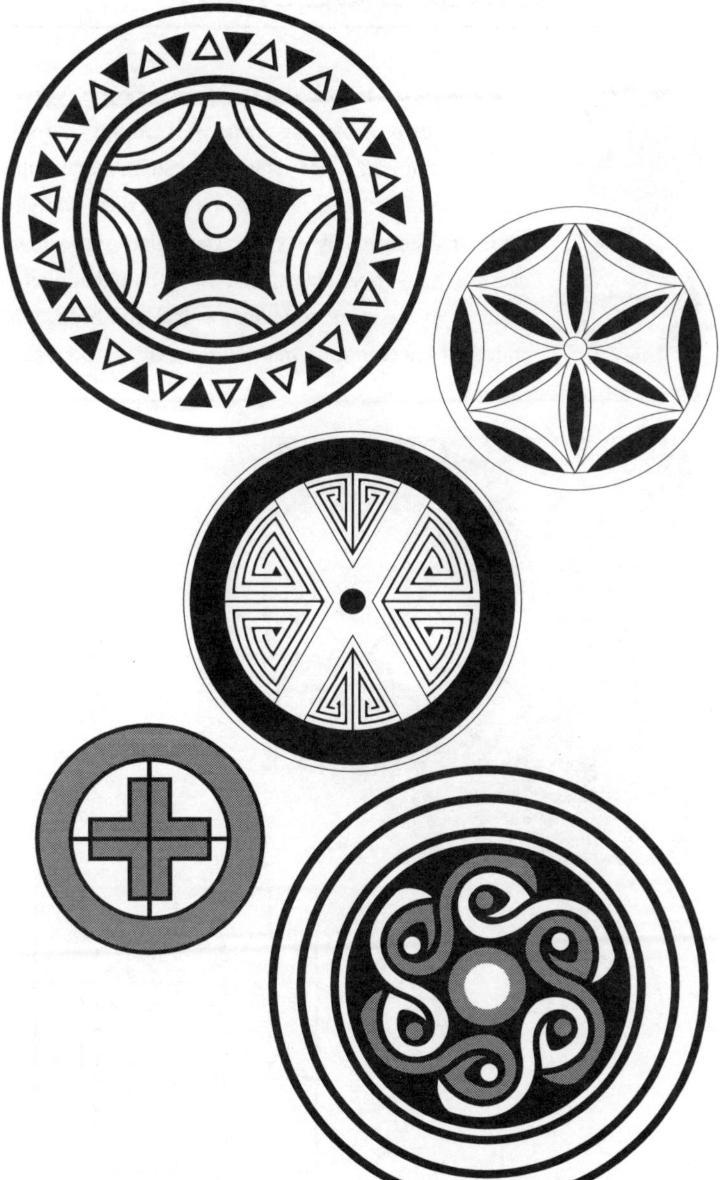

Step Patterns

Step patterns arrived in the Celtic repertoire before the imported Bibles, but almost certainly derived from the same classical source, presumably through trade. They were used much as circle designs were, to fill in areas, especially corners. The artists of the manuscripts and cross slabs used their simplicity as a contrast to the more complex vertical and horizontal panels of knotwork, animal interlace or key patterns.

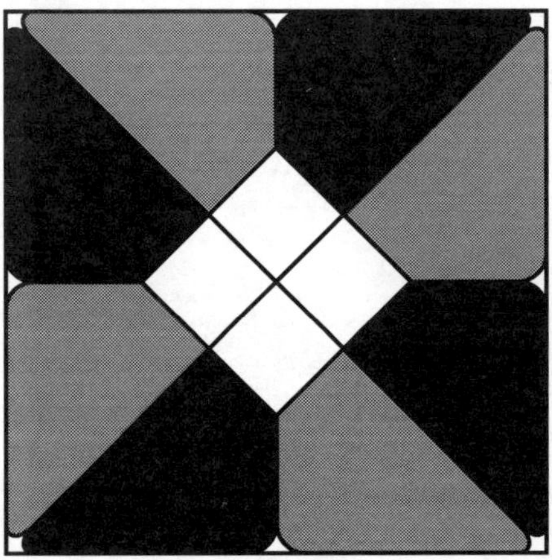

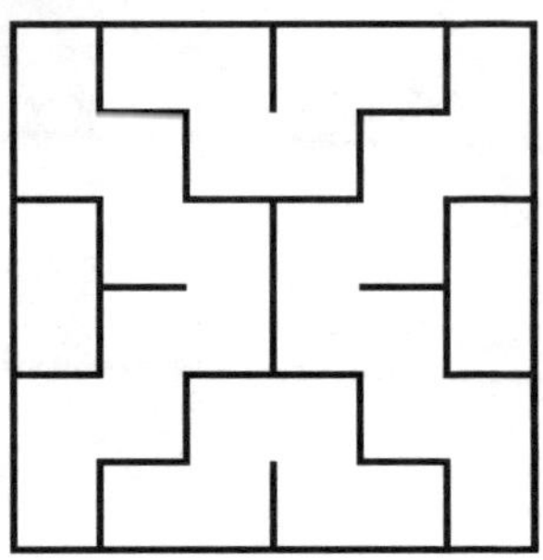

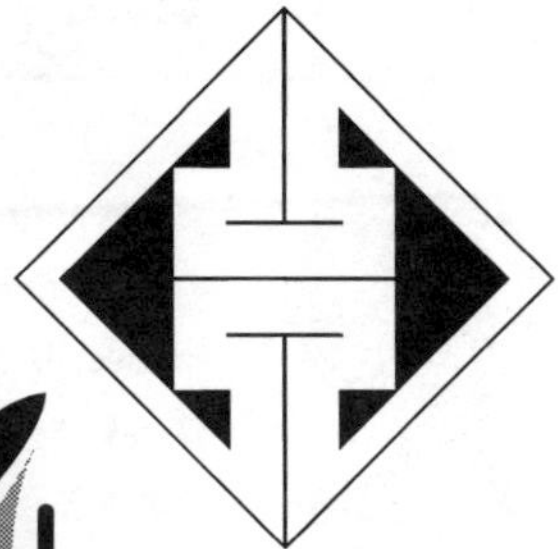

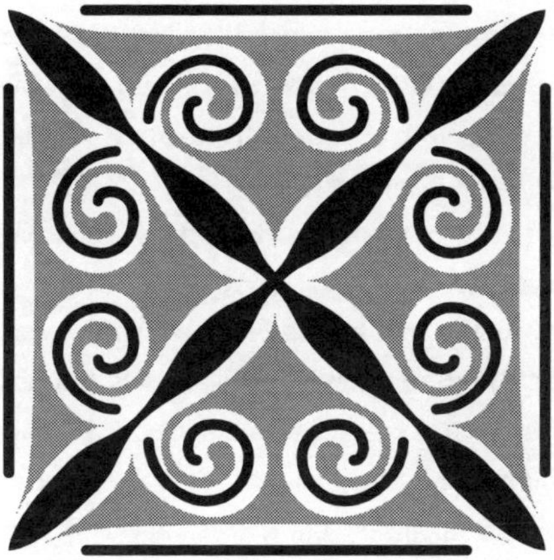

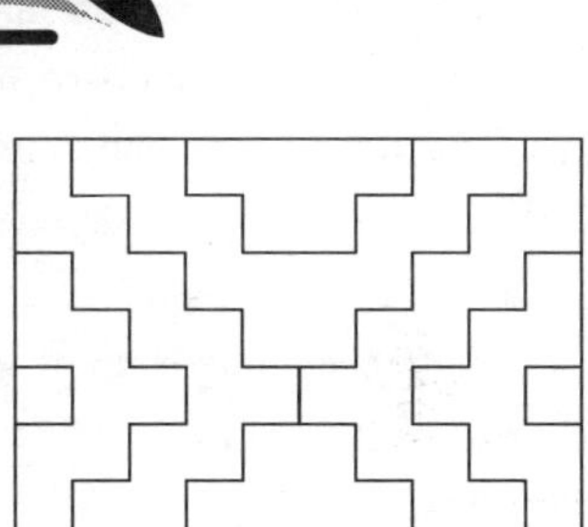

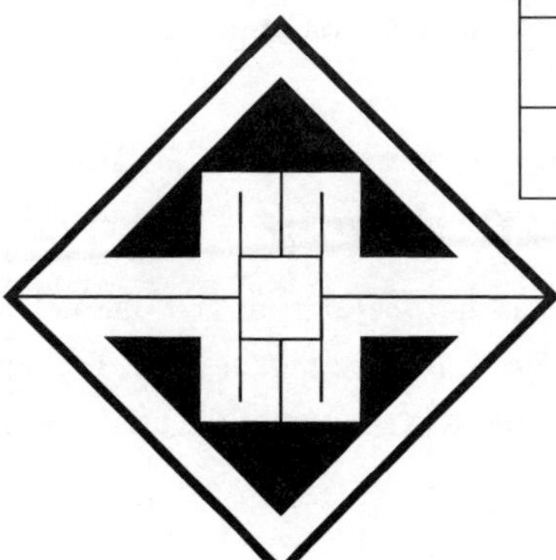

key patterns

Key patterns are simply square versions of the Celts' favourite motif – the spiral. From archaeological evidence, it seems that they developed separately from the Greek fret patterns with which they have often been linked. The two are similar, but by using their traditional diagonal grid, the Celts ended up with a version that allowed a lot more variation than the Greek and Roman square-grid.

As in most Celtic art, the balance between areas of different colours is both vital and delicate. In the case of key patterns, the two areas are almost identical, so the eye has to work out which is the background and which the foreground. Whichever line is thinner is perceived to be the foreground, so if you want to make one set of lines or one colour stand out, make those lines slightly thinner. The thicker line, though actually taking up more space, will appear to recede into the background. If the two lines are exactly the same, and the colours chosen are bright and contrasting, an optical illusion is created, with the eye jumping from one line to the other.

To draw a key pattern start with a grid (we will use a square grid to simplify the process) made up of squares of units. In this example we have a row of five 10 by 10 grids. You may use printed grid paper to simplify the process

how to draw key patterns

1. First draw the diagonals, starting one unit up and one unit in from the bottom corner to one unit from the top edge. The next diagonal starts two units along from the end of the previous line and one up from the bottom.

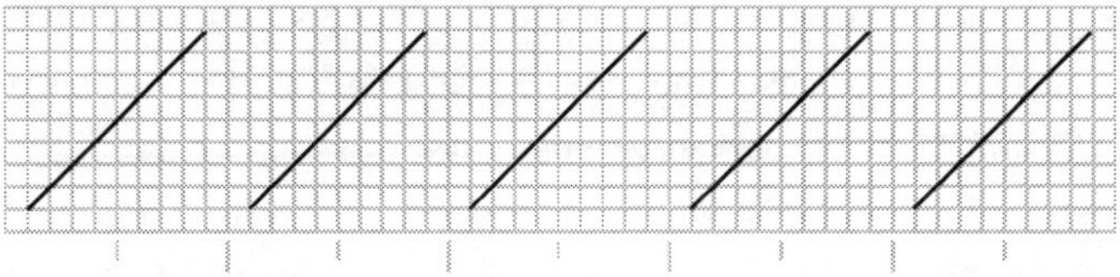

2. Next draw the opposite diagonals, again starting and finishing one unit from the edge. This time leave a unit square clear between the lines, so that they are at least one diagonal unit apart.

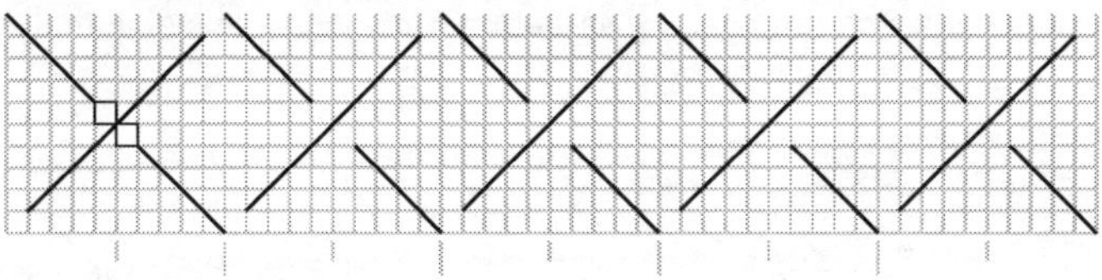

3. Now the lines all start to spiral inwards, turning through a right-angle in towards the centre, each stopping one diagonal unit away from the others.

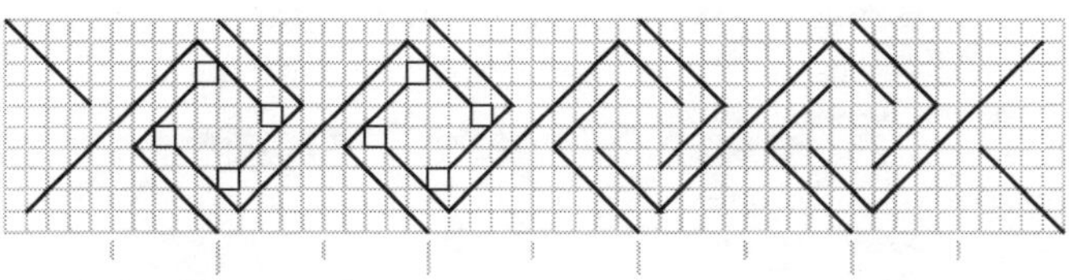

4. Do the same again, noticing that the lines are getting shorter with each turn.

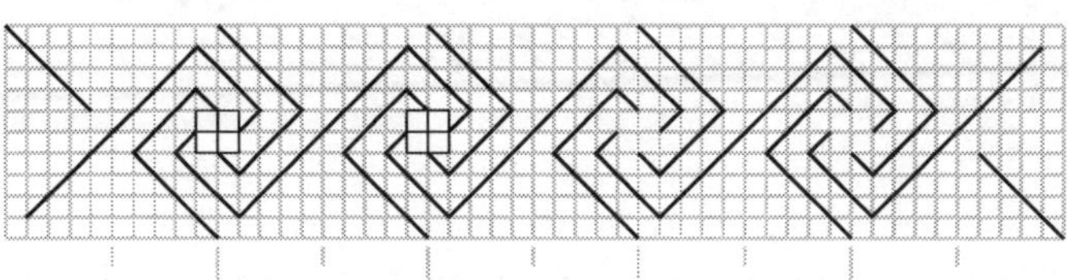

5. Now that the central portion of the pattern is basically finished, it is time to complete the edges. Because they started with a diagonal grid, the Celts had to work out a new way of finishing off the edges when the key pattern was in a square or rectangular area. They came up with the unique triangular edges that make Celtic key patterns look totally different from all other forms of fret pattern. First the long outside horizontals and verticals are drawn in from the ends of the unbroken diagonals. As with all the other lines, they stop as soon as they get to one diagonal unit away from the next line.

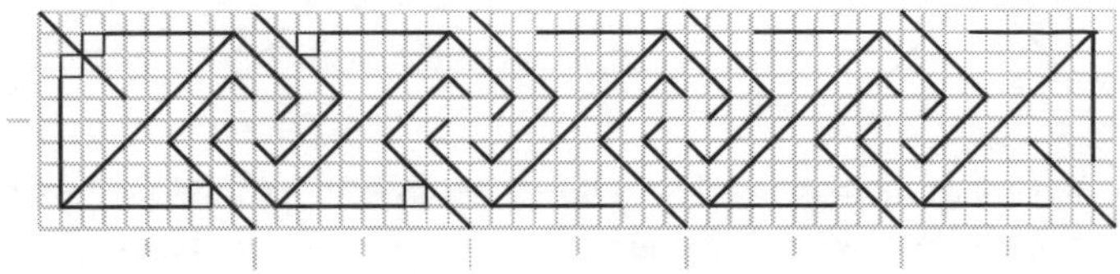

6. This space can be filled with three different triangles, but the first of those shown below was almost always used.

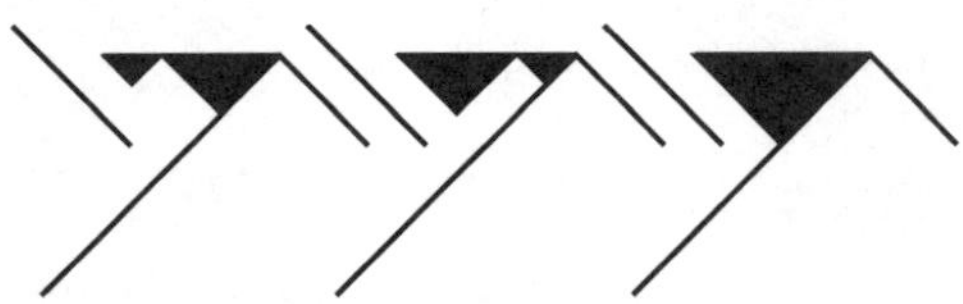

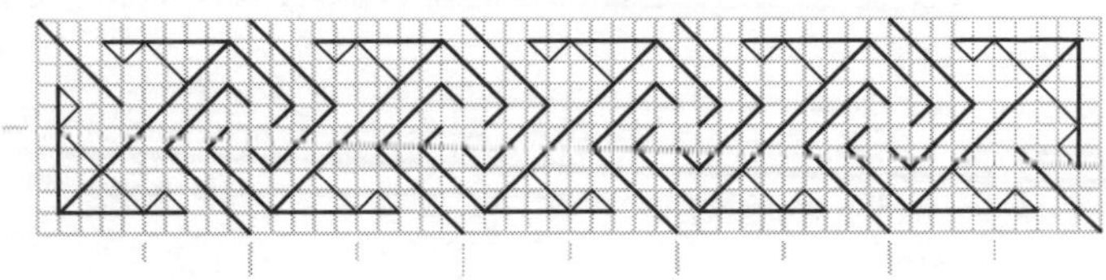

7. This allows the addition of one more short line to fill in the space left by the triangles. As usual it stops one diagonal unit away from the next line (in this case the triangles), so no part of the pattern is nearer or further than one diagonal unit away from the others.

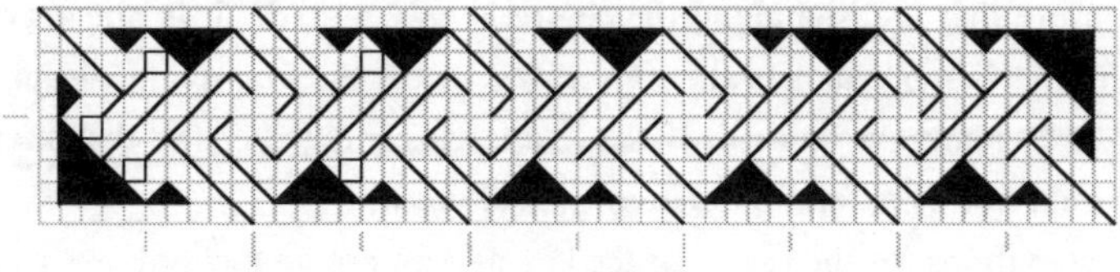

8. Finally we add the rectangular frame, and there you have it: a complete key pattern. As mentioned above, the lines can be thickened until they are as wide as the gap between them or even wider to make the white lines stand out.

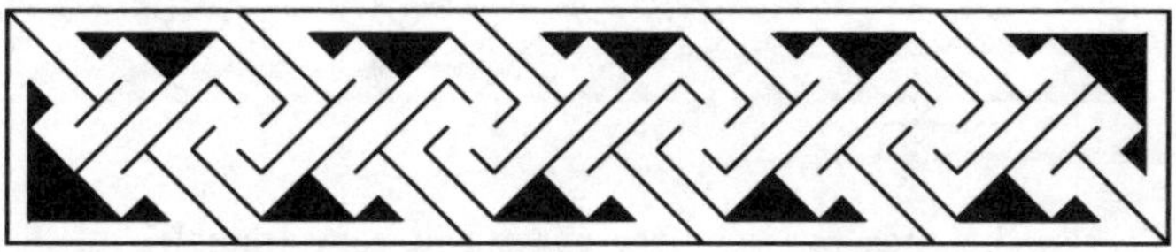

Many variations can be made on the centre of the key pattern. As with every design they created, Celtic artists used as many variations on the basic pattern as they could come up with.

There is the problem of how to fill an area larger than a single border. The answer is simple: copy the pattern above or below the previous one so that the diagonals that reach the edges meet.

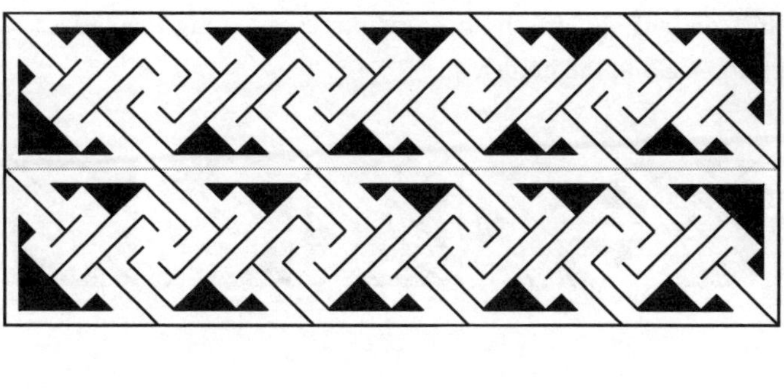

Note that the line along the centre is only a guide. It is not linked in, and is more or less the only place where the one-diagonal-apart rule is routinely ignored. If they were closer together the diagonals would not meet, and the pattern would skew.

Variations for the centre of the key pattern are limited only by your imagination. Here are a few of the more common ones.

The ends of the lines can be joined up in any way you can think of.

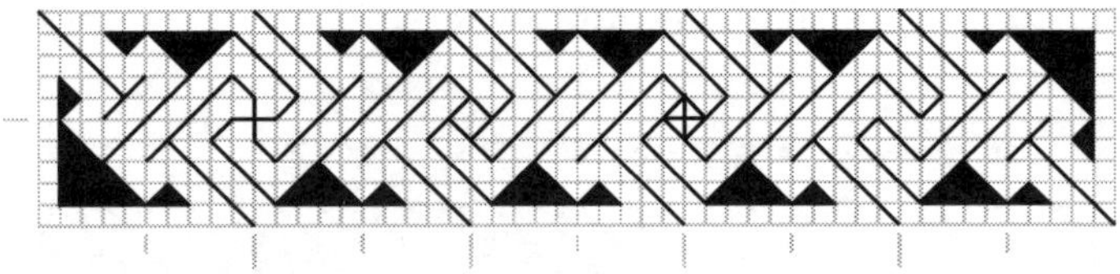

Or else the ends can echo the edges and have triangles on them, either horizontal or vertical.

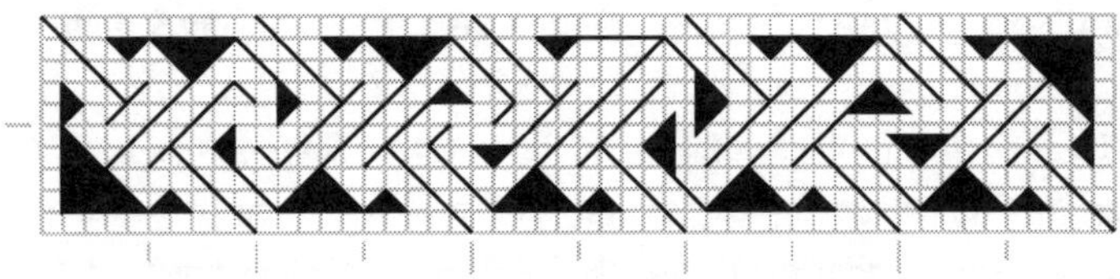

These triangles can be enlarged or divided into smaller triangles until you end up with the two end pieces repeating themselves back and forth along the border.

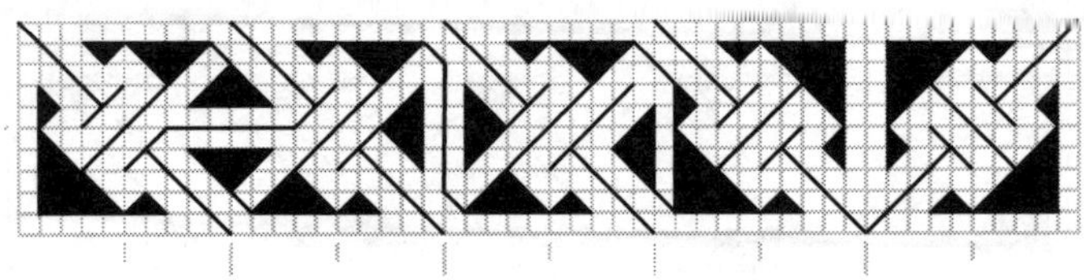

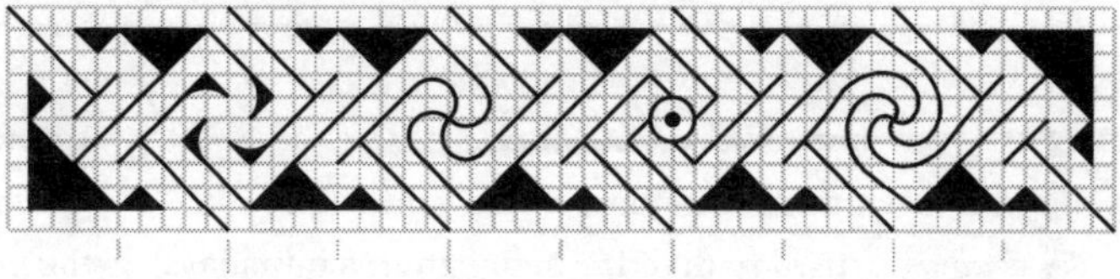

Finally the original nature of the design can be brought back, and the lines can end in proper curved spirals, circles or any other shape you like.

Key pattern borders are usually seen as tattooed armbands, and they are very suitable for this use. It seems a shame that they are almost always plain black. Given the Celts' love of colour and the pain of tattooing, it is a pity not to go for the brilliance and vitality of the enamels and manuscripts. In body painting you can experiment with different colours to see which suit your eyes, hair and clothes. But remember, black is for outlines, not for fillings.

knotwork

Knotwork, or interlace (which is strictly speaking different, though the term 'knotwork' is generally used to describe both patterns nowadays), is the most immediately recognizable of all Celtic artwork, even though it seems to have been invented fairly late in the history of the Celts. By rotating the grid used for drawing classical interlace patterns through 45°, the Celts discovered a new world of variations with infinite possibilities. Unlike their classical predecessors, the innovative Celts experimented with the permutations of the knots themselves and with different ways of finishing the designs. They drew scores of different knots in the last few centuries of Celtic art, and it has taken further centuries to unravel the techniques they used. Luckily for us, they left millions of knots for us to investigate.

The symbolic meaning of knots has never been committed to paper (or vellum), so we can only guess at it. The links with symbols from other cultures (such as the Tree of Life and the World Snake) seem fairly obvious. These imply that knotwork represented the cycle of life and death, and the interconnectedness of all creation that was a basic belief shared by the Celts and the early Christians.

There are good reasons to believe that drawing and studying knotwork were used as a form of contemplative meditation. The years of practice required to become a master draughtsman in Celtic knotwork would have echoed the years of study required to become a druid, and it may well be that drawing knotwork and other symbols was part of this training. The complexity of knotwork requires a great deal of concentration and attention to detail, while the simple geometry allows the artist or viewer to empty his or her mind of the distractions of the outside world.

The traditional method of designing knotwork takes years of study and copying to master. The following instructions are not based on the methods used by Celtic scribes, but have been greatly simplified so that you can get started on designing your own knotwork as quickly as possible.

How to Draw Knotwork

This method does not use the diagonal grid pattern that give Celtic knotwork and key patterns their distinctive look and potential for variation. It is a method designed for the modern artist, so it is drawn on the square grid that we seem to find easier to work with.

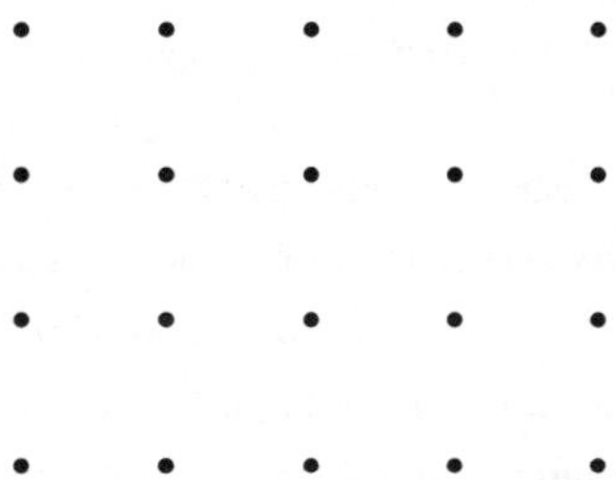

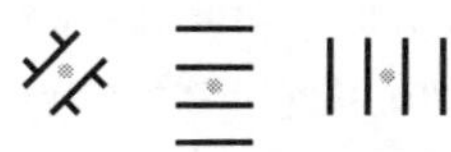

1. Divide up the area you want to fill (either a complete knot or a repeatable section) into as many units as you think necessary for the scale and complexity of your design. Using a pencil, fill the area with a grid of dots, one unit apart.

   The joy of this system is that it is based on just three ‘pieces’. These are the crossover points, to be centred on the dots of your grid, and from these simple sets of lines all regular Celtic knotwork can be drawn. Taking the space between your dots as one unit, the lines are one-quarter of a unit apart, and one-eighth of a unit from the top and bottom or sides of the grid lines. For a fuller explanation of this system, see my earlier book, How to Draw Celtic Knotwork: A Practical Handbook.

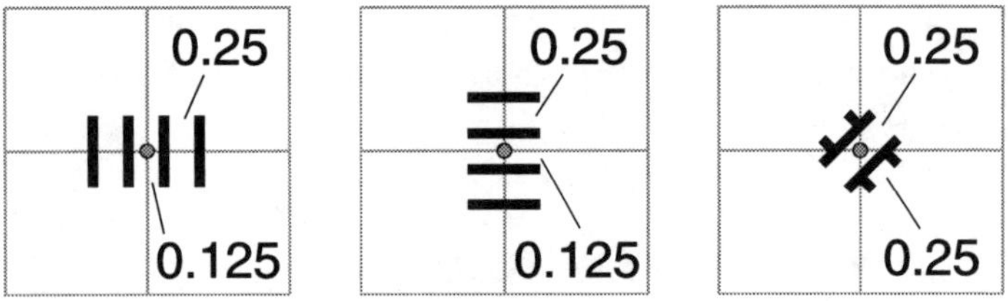

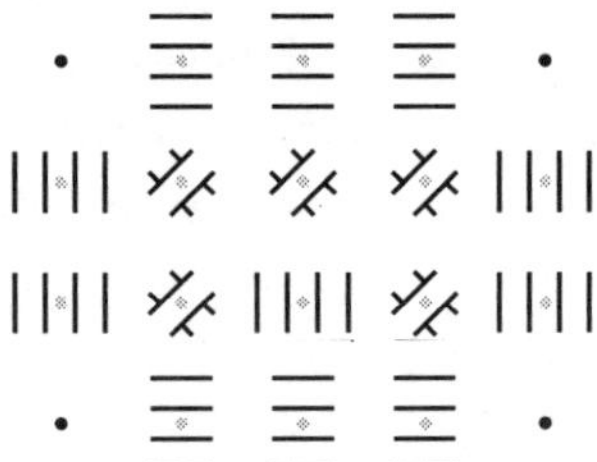

2. Now pencil in one of the three pieces around each of the dots. The outer edges must be horizontal or vertical pieces, but the insides can be anything you like. Leave the corner pieces, as we will deal with them later. You must draw all the diagonal pieces going the same way, otherwise the 'over and under' of true Celtic knotwork will be lost.

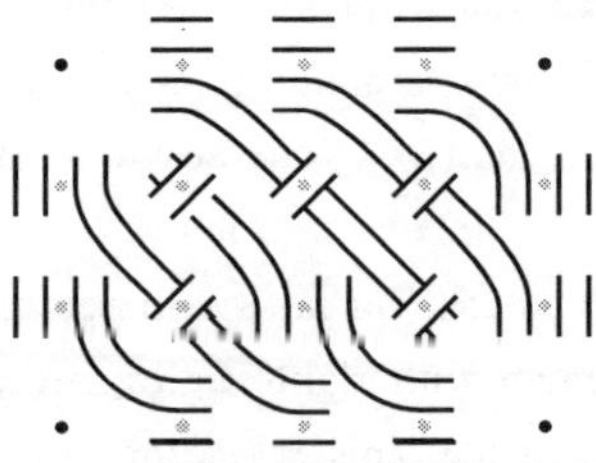

3. Next, extend the ends of the lines to join up, from the top left to the bottom right. Complete all of these (except where the lack of corners stops you) before moving on to the next stage.

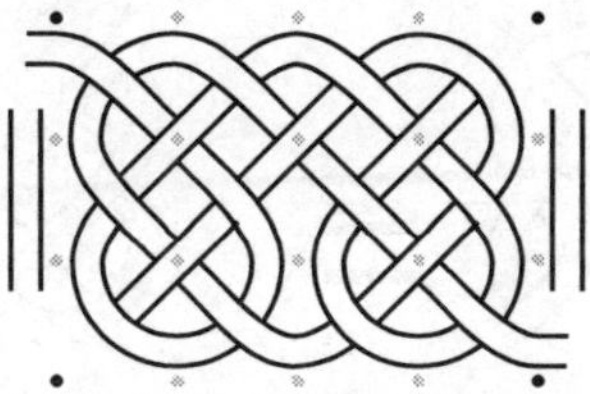

4 Having done this, you can now draw in the lines from top right to bottom left. As you can see, these all go under the lines drawn in the last step (except at the diagonal pieces), so care must be taken that the broken curves look smooth.

Notice that the extra lines along the edges have been erased, as they are not needed for a closed knot.

We now have our basic knot shape. The corners have been left unfinished because the knot can go either of two ways now, becoming either a closed knot or a repeatable unit in a knotwork border.

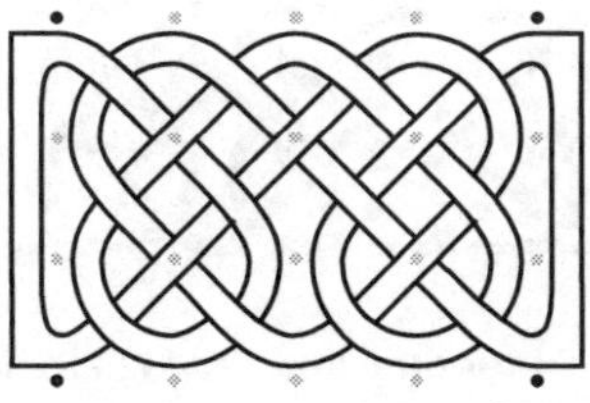

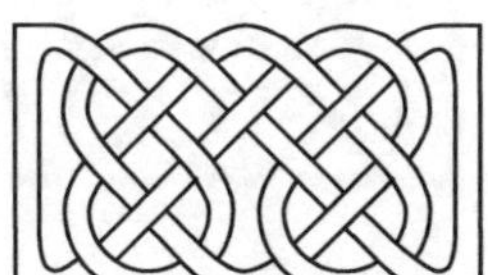

5 To make a closed knot, you have to join up all the loose ends. This is very straightforward, as you can see in the diagram. Notice how the corners are drawn with right-angles on the outer edge and curves on the inner edge. This is one of the hallmarks of Celtic knotwork, and looks much more authentic than rounded or square corners. And there you have a finished knot.

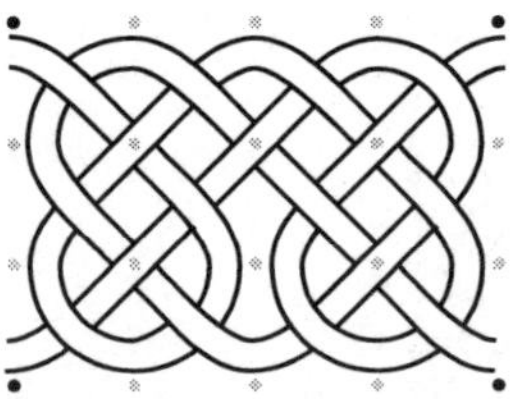

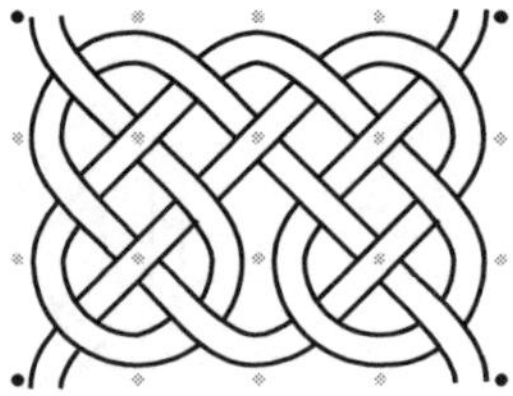

6. If you want the knot to be a repeatable unit, the ends must stay open. This means that the separate lines and the right and left-hand ends can be erased. The loose ends of the knot can now be finished by putting in a normal vertical or horizontal connection, depending on the way you want to connect the knots.

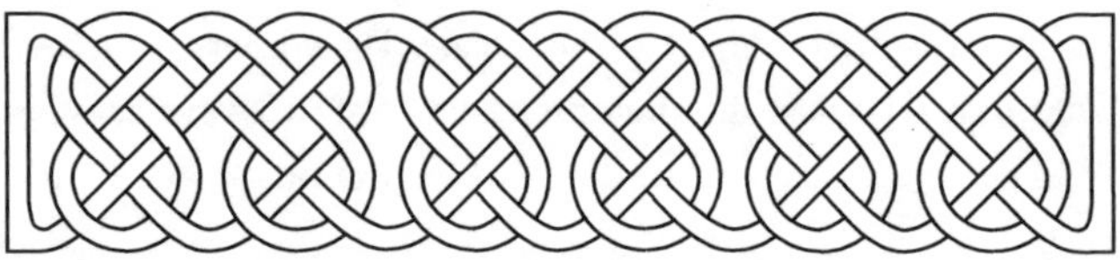

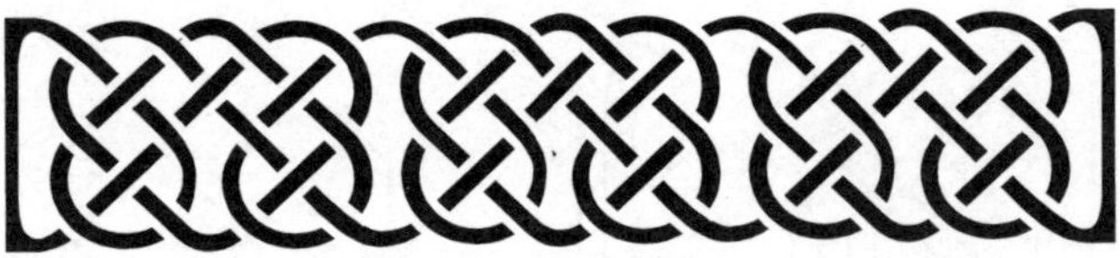

Knotwork bands or borders are ideal for armbands and ankle-bands. To make a continuous band where the cords meet each other, first measure your arm or leg. Then enlarge or reduce the design (photocopiers that enlarge by percentage are useful here) that you want until it is the required length and copy it onto the skin.

The following knot comes from the Book of Lindisfarne.

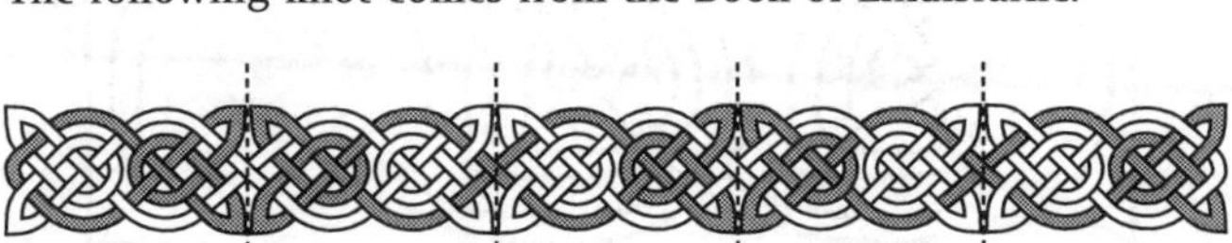

The next two knots come from the Book of Durrow. The second design was used to fill an area, but there is no reason not to use it as a band, especially in connection with more Gothic images.

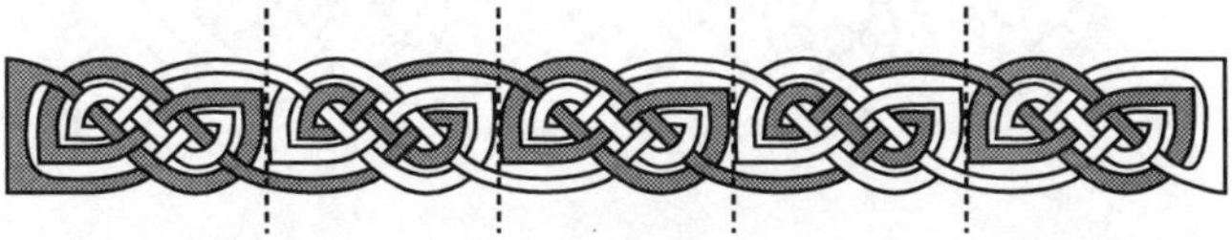

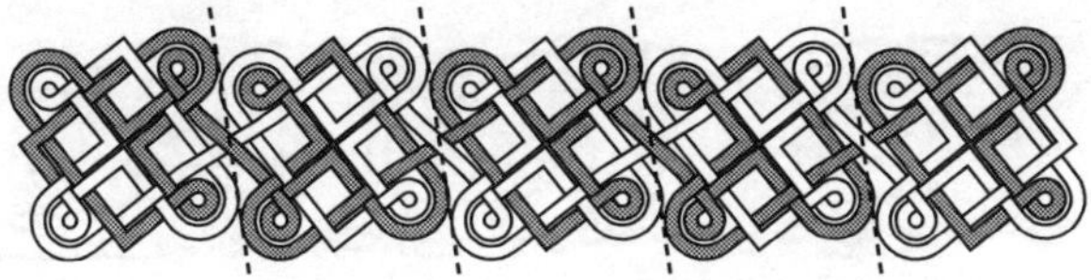

The following knot comes from the Collieburn stone, where it is used as a single unit. Once again, it can easily be made into a band.

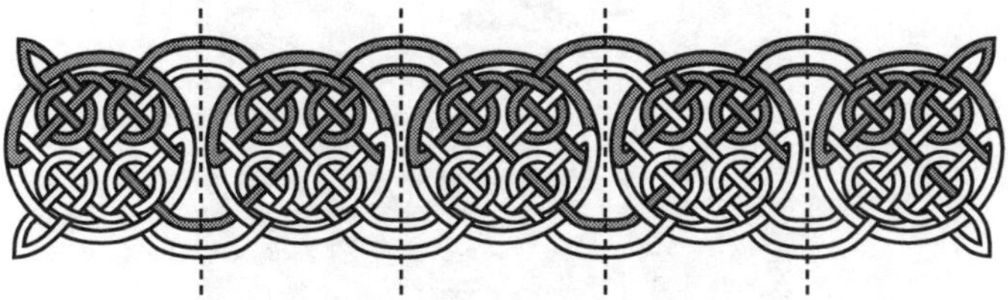

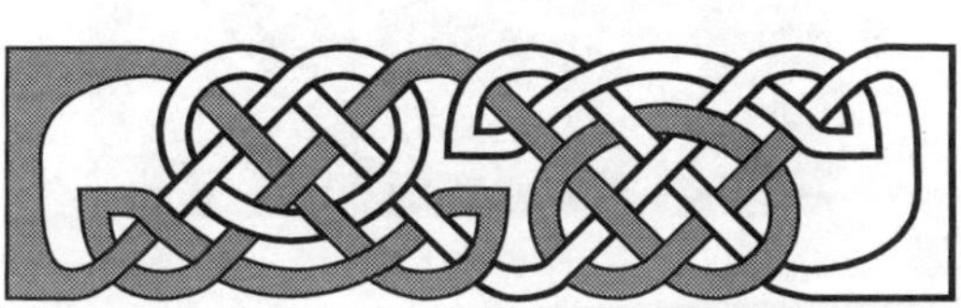

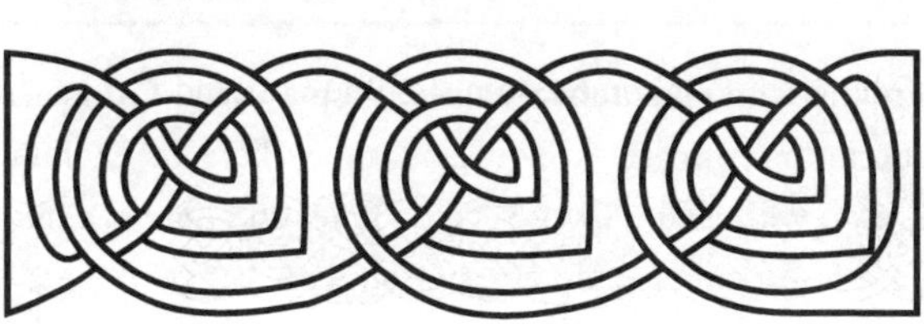

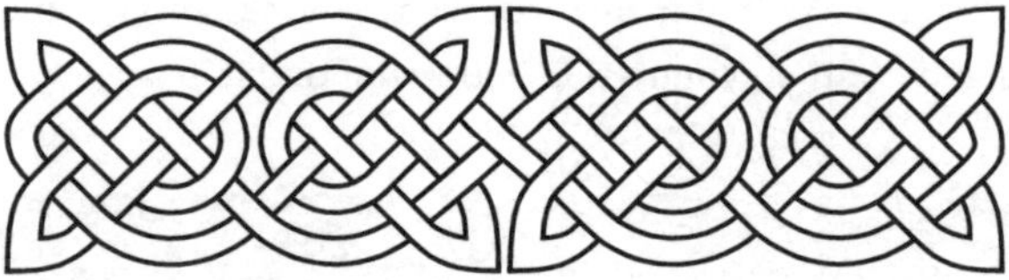

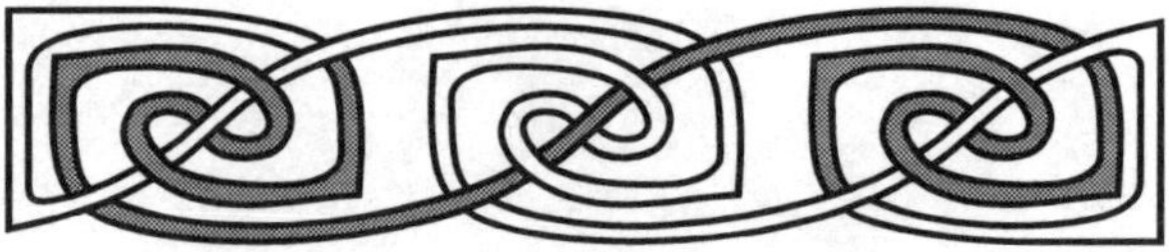

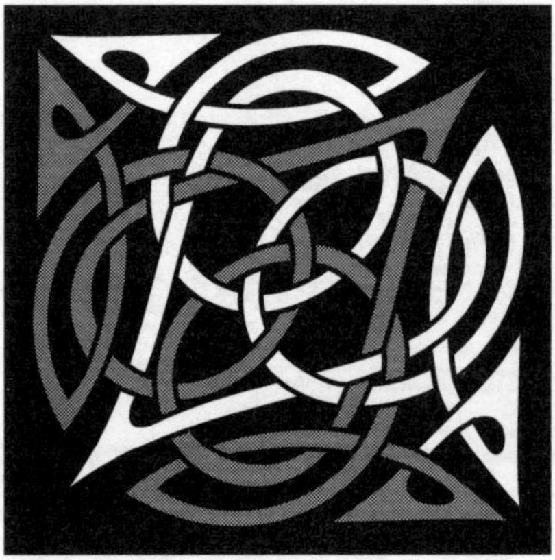

Circular knotwork is probably more appropriate for general body decoration. Unfortunately there isn't space here to explain how to draw it. You will need a more specific book on knotwork for that, but here are a few examples to be going on with.

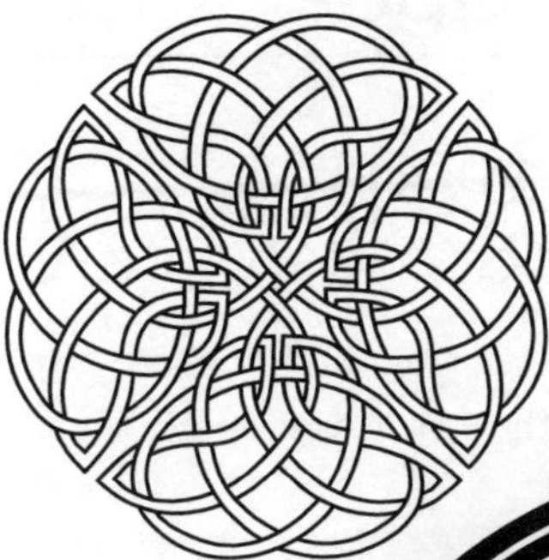

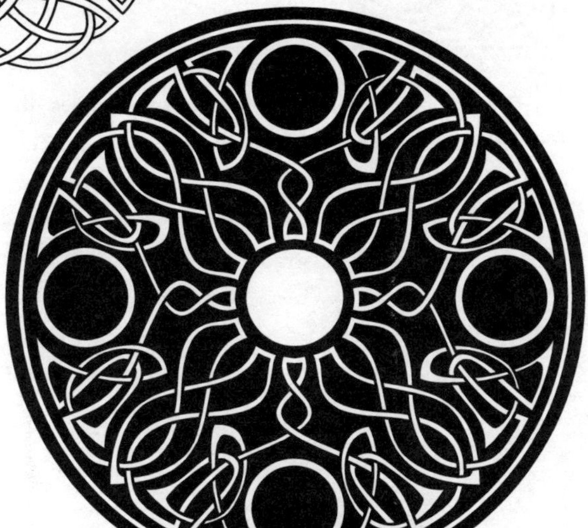

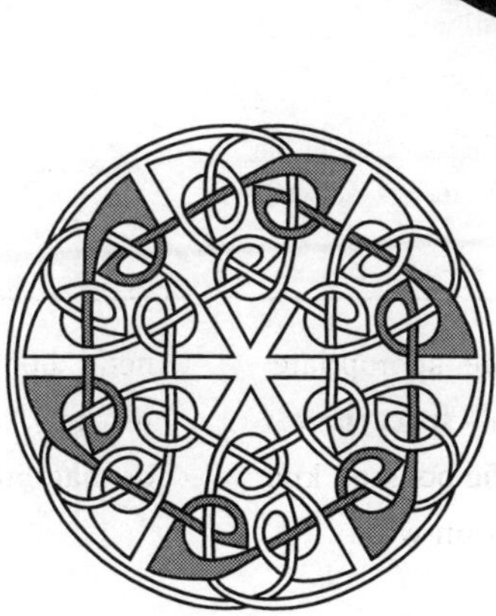

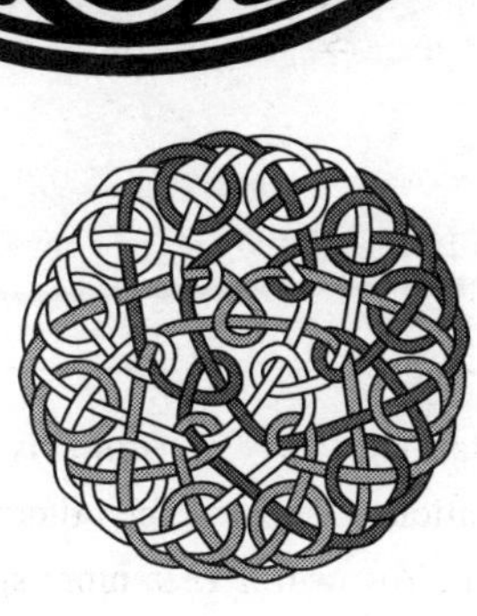

Snake Images

How to Draw Snake Images

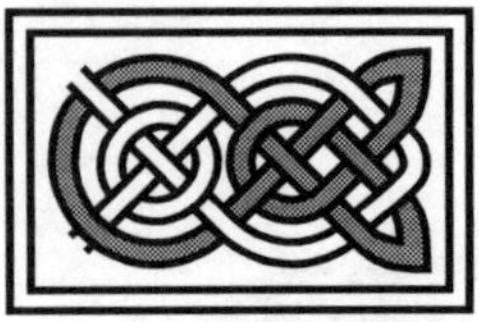

Take your piece of knotwork and give it two loose ends. These should preferably be in a corner.

1. Starting with the head, draw two circles to almost fill in the area you have to work in. The centre of each circle is the end of one edge of the knotwork strand, and they have the same radius as the width of the strand.

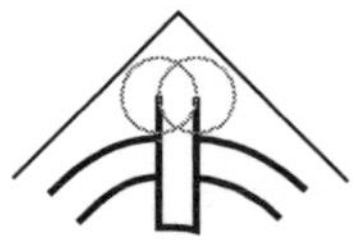

2. Draw two more circles half the size inside one of these circles.

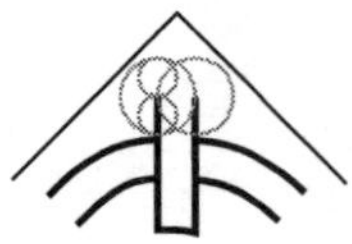

3. Inside the top circle draw two more concentric circles, then ink in the lines as shown.

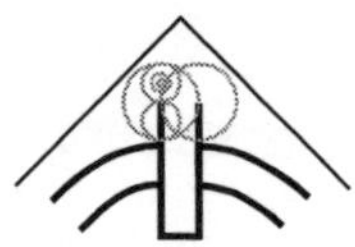

4. Add a V shape to the eye. Repeat in the opposite circle.

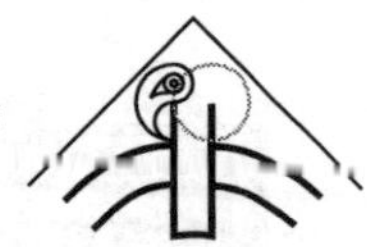

5. Now for the nose. Draw two lines from the eye-pieces towards the edge of the border.

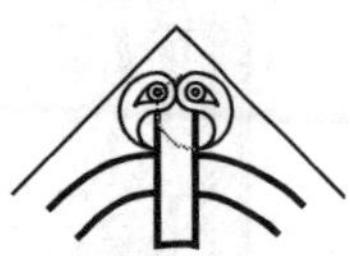

6. Join these with two lines parallel to the border lines.

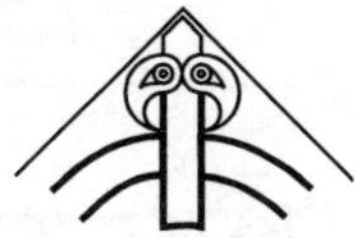

7. Finally put the ridge down the middle of the nose and add some nostrils.

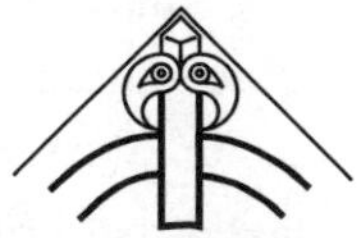

The knot lines usually stop at the eyes, so the head looks bigger. The eyes may be extended to fill space and the snake may have a tongue.

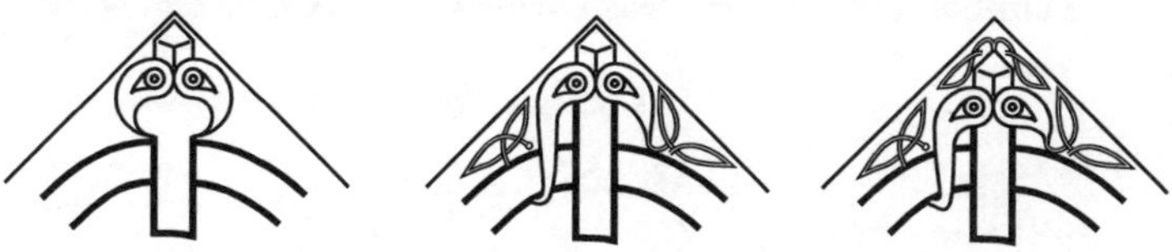

8. Now the tail. Draw an arc centred on the corner.

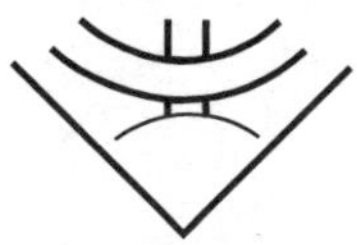

9. Join the ends with smaller arcs. There are four here, but two is just as common, with the centre pointing well into the corner.

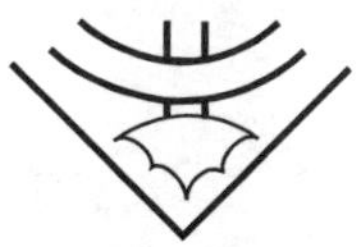

10. Finally, draw the ridges. And there you have a finished snake knot.

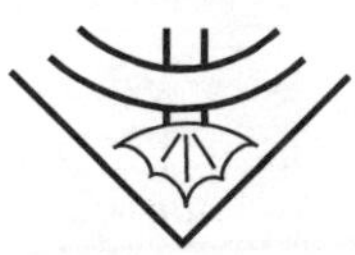

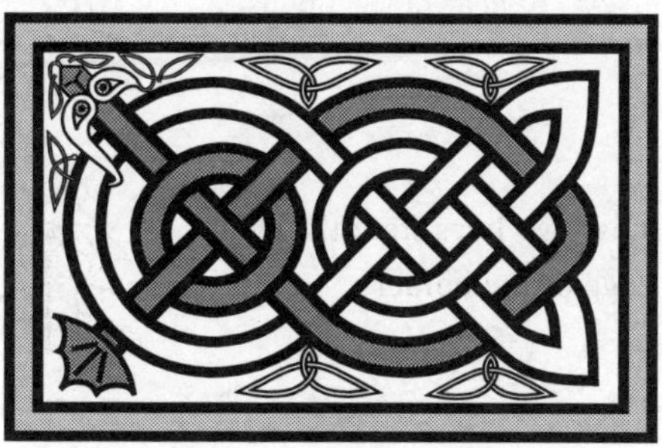

Icons of Celtic Art

Possibly the most famous birds in Celtic mythology are the three daughters of Lir, who were turned into swans, only returning to their human forms when a prophesy was fulfilled three centuries later. There are innumerable other references to birds throughout Celtic mythology, each species having a different significance. Crows and ravens, for instance, symbolize death, and swans nobility and purity, while eagles are the lords of the air, taking on all the attributes of heroism. Owls are the outcasts of the bird world.

kells

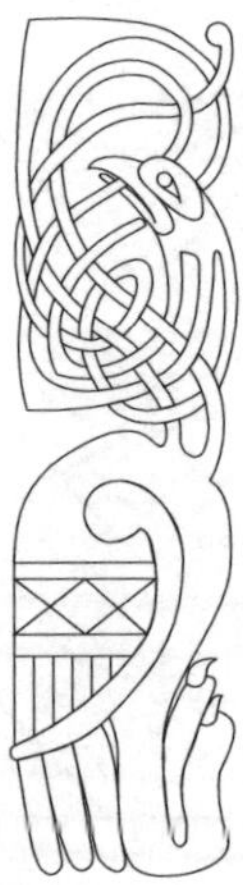

Lindisfarne

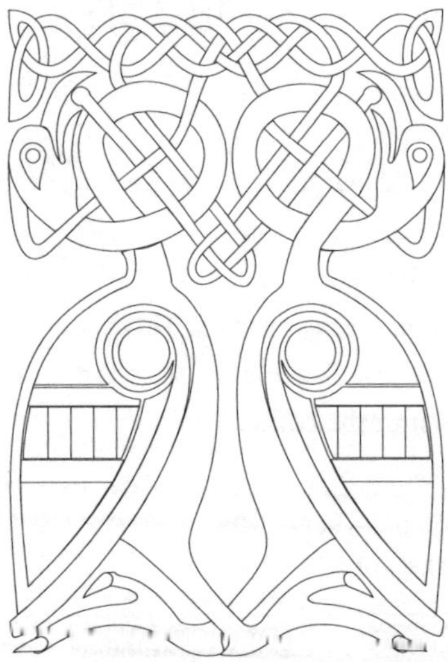

kells

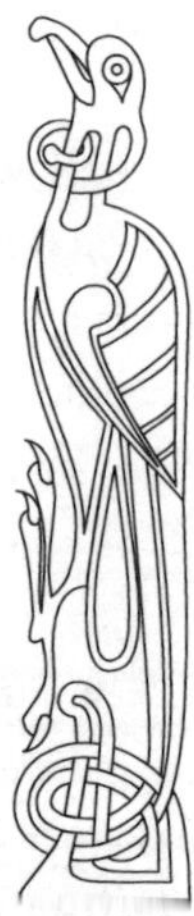

kells

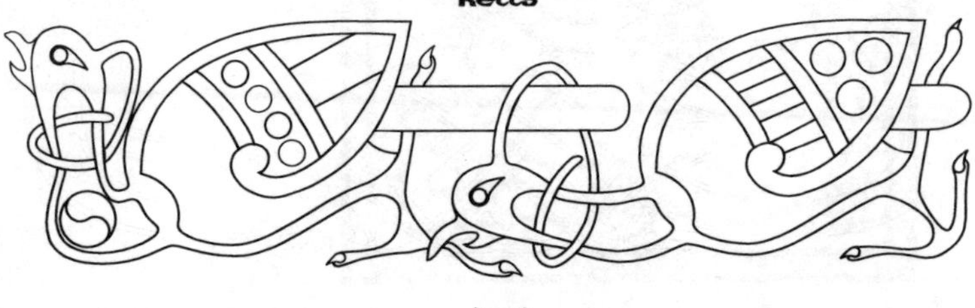

Lindisfarne

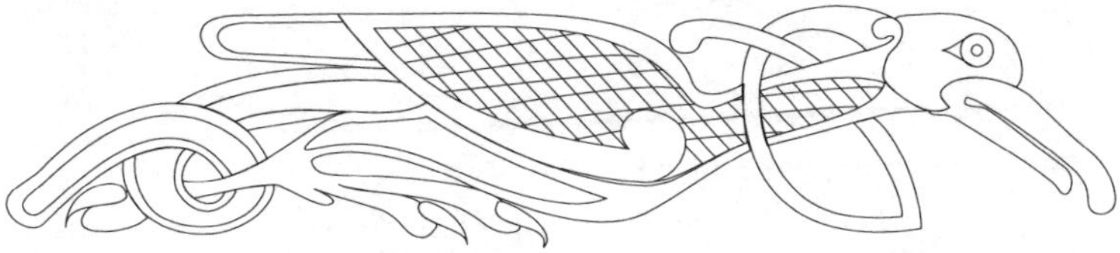

Kells

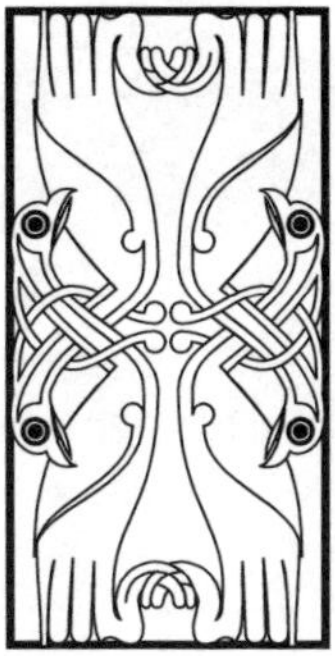

All Celtic bird symbolism seems to have come from a common source, as there are many similarities in its use, despite wide variations in design. Celtic artists apparently took to birds more than any other zoomorph. No images of birds have been found from the pre-Christian Celtic world, and those from the golden age of Celtic art all seem to be either of peacocks (from the look of their plumage) or of cormorants and other sea-birds. This is because sea-birds, having links with the elements of water, earth and air, were regarded as special. And, of course, the scribes drew their inspiration from the birds they saw around them, on the sea-cliffs and shores where they lived.

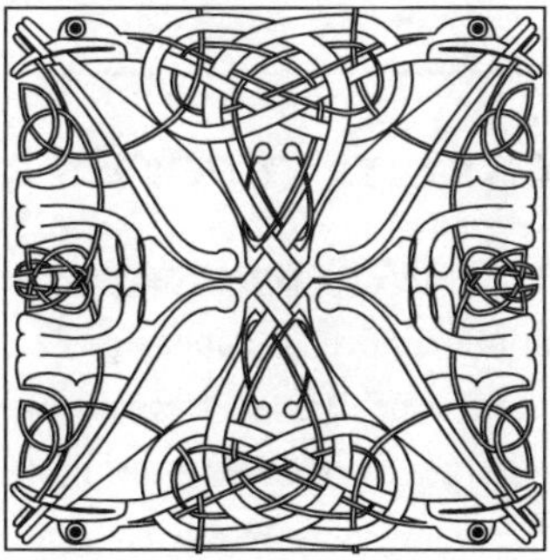

Lichfield

Kells

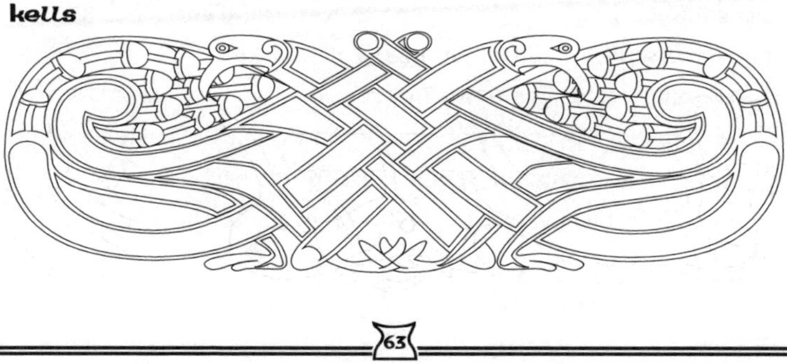

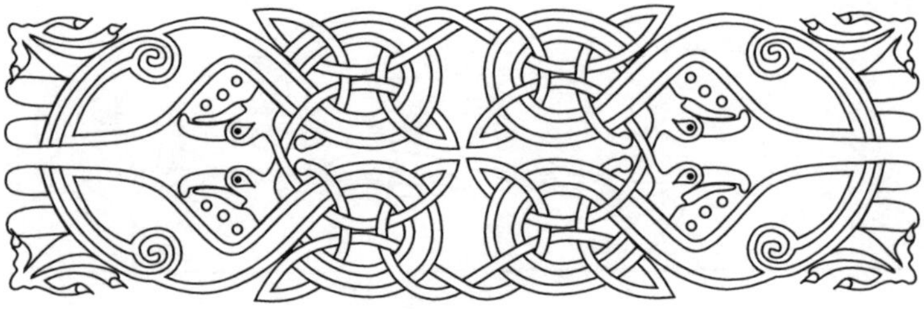

Common points in bird drawings

The birds' heads were always very similar. It was in the body that variations tended to appear.

The beak was always drawn with a small lower half and a large, curving, overhanging top half.

The eyes were always drawn in the same way as the snake's: two concentric circles with a V shape coming from the larger.

The topknot always came from the back of the head, its length depending on how much space had to be filled. If there was a lot of space, the scribe would often extend it into knotwork or whatever shape would fit the area to be filled.

The edge of the wing was always shown, but the circle denoting the shoulder is usually further up, closer to the neck.

The tail feathers varied in number from one to about five, and

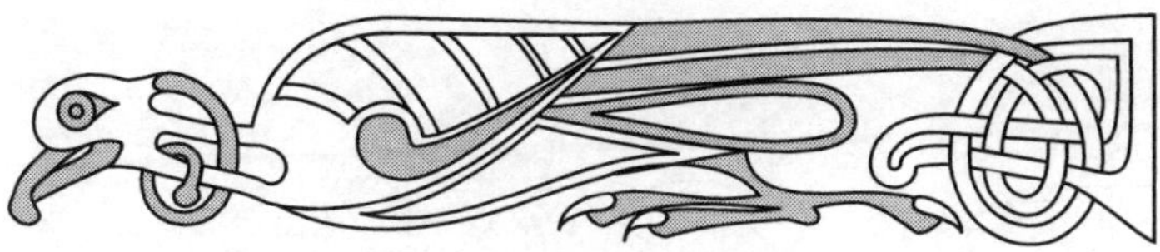

their length was again dependent on the space to be filled. In some images the feathers are all the same size, usually short, while in others, such as this one, one feather is short and the others long. Tail feathers were the element most commonly extended into knotwork (as in this design) and in a border design often interlace with the neck of the bird behind.

The feet were almost always drawn as shown here: two talons, thin at the heel and bulging towards the end, one to the front and one to the back, with curving tear-shaped claws.

Dog Images

As you can see from the examples, there are few similarities between images of dogs in the illuminated manuscripts other than the universal eyes and feet. This implies that although the dog was a very important animal to the Celts, there was little or no history of drawing it. The fact that there are so many dog designs in illuminated manuscripts hints at how Christianity changed when it reached northern Britain. Generally in the Bible dogs are shown in a very poor light, yet to the Celts (and in Celtic Christianity) dogs were an important and almost sacred animal, denoting faithfulness, obedience to duty and prowess at hunting – all of which talents and qualities were cornerstones of Celtic culture.

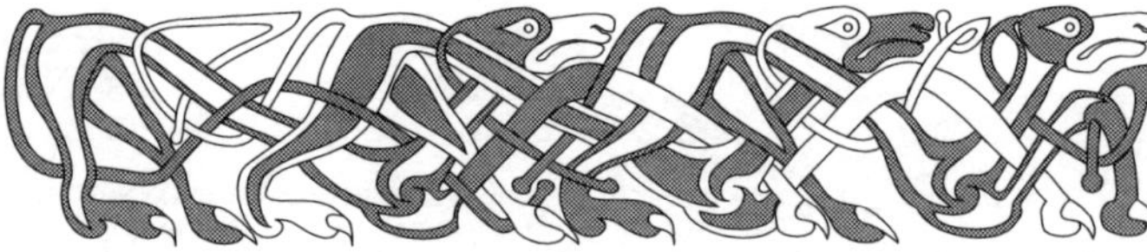

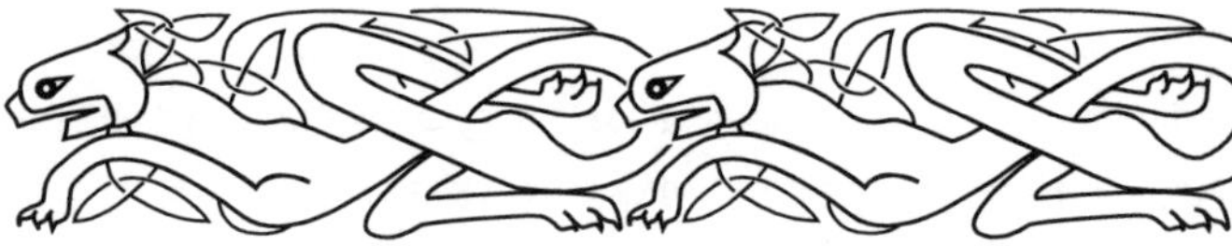

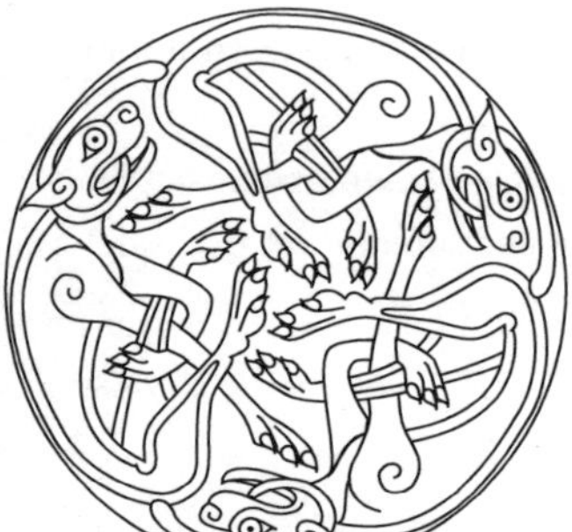

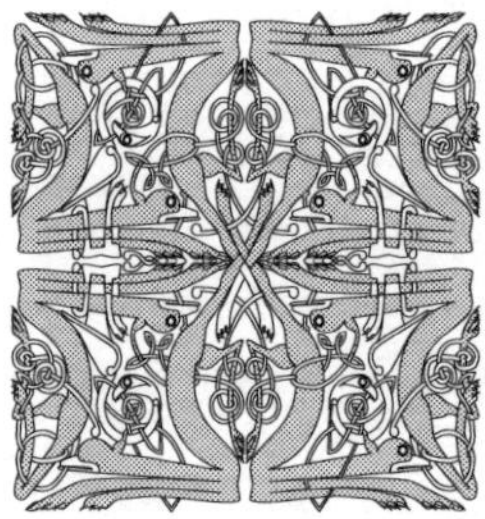

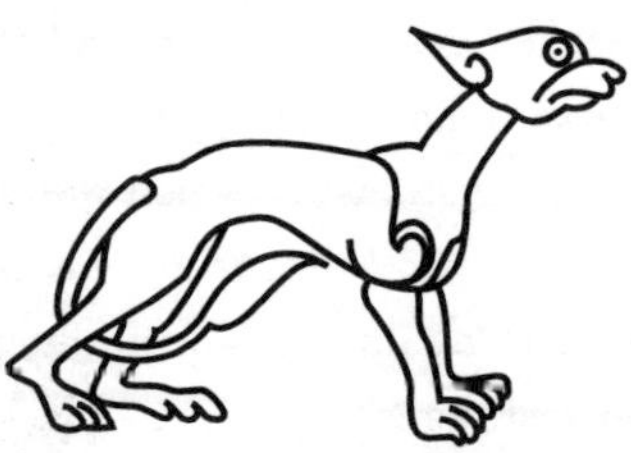

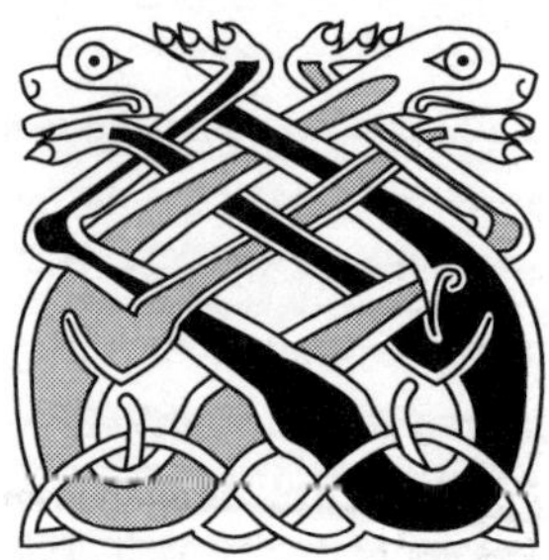

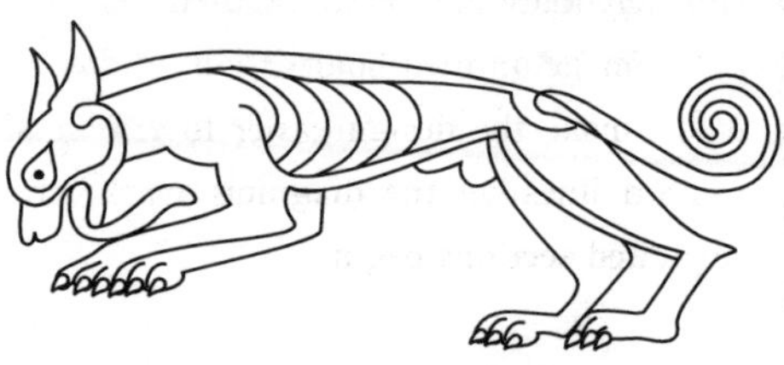

tree of life

This is the name given by George Bain to the Celtic variation on the classical vine pattern. It is not a traditional Celtic pattern, nor a common or widespread one. There do not appear to be any pre-Christian examples in the Celtic world, but some do appear in the Book of Kells and on carved stones in southern Pictland (south-east Scotland and Northumberland), so the pattern would have been available for use around the time of Isidore of Seville's reference to Pictish body art.

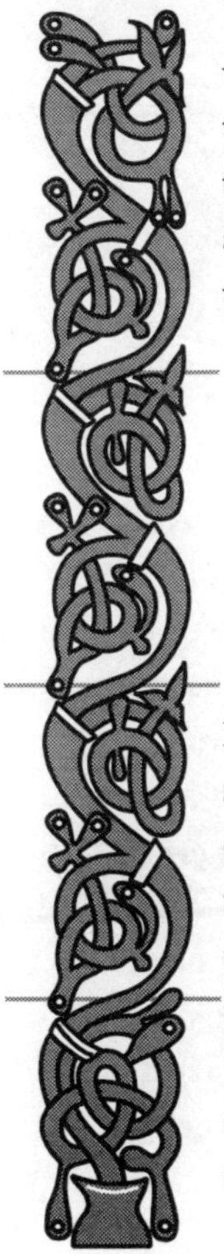

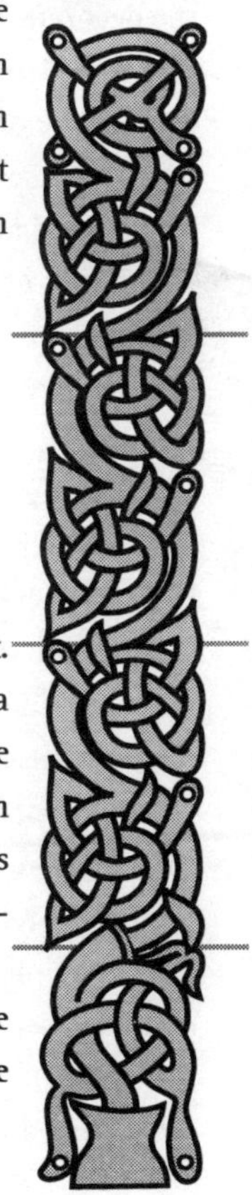

Tree of life designs start with a pot for the vine to grow in (like the Asian rather than the classical models, though they are drawn to a different basic design). Celts almost always used a branching spiral rather than the classical pattern shown below.

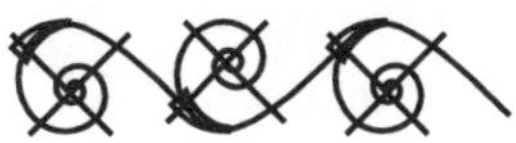

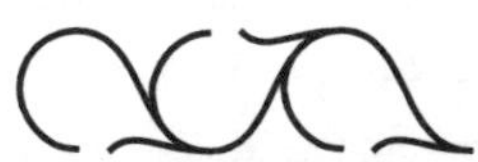

Only two examples of this design exist. Both are in the Book of Kells, which has a strong Christian association. There was some exchange of symbols and images between the Pagans and the Christians, but it is unlikely that the Picts would used such a foreign image on their bodies.

To make the design easier to follow, the dotted lines on the diagrams mark where repeated sections begin.

people

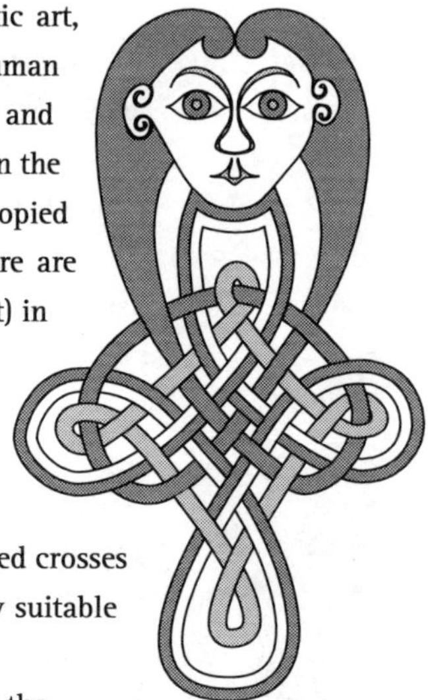

Book of kells

As we saw in the section on early Celtic art, there is a long tradition of drawing human beings or heads attached to knotwork and interlace ornament. While the portraits in the illuminated manuscripts are obviously copied from Byzantine originals, the men (there are no women except Mary in any Celtic art) in the decorations derive much more from this early Celtic heritage. As with the Tree of Life designs, the greatest number of these images comes from the Northumbrian manuscripts and the carved crosses of the east of Scotland, so they are very suitable for Pictish body art.

Faces are almost always drawn in the same way: with almond-shaped eyes and circular pupils. Portrait faces are usually drawn as in the cross figure in the illustration from the Book of Kells, and the profiles are similar. Hair was often intertwined and spiralled, but never showed the tonsures of the Columban and Augustine monks who drew the images. It was sometimes extended to fill an empty space with knotwork, like the topknots on the birds. The same is true of beards, which seem to be included only when there is an area to be filled with knotwork. For some reason, when a beard is included it is usually held in one hand by the wearer. In Celtic thinking fair hair was good, dark hair bad.

As with all the other zoomorphic designs, the body could be twisted into whatever shape had to be filled as long as it remained recognizable. A lot of practice is required to develop your own designs, but the results are well worth the effort.

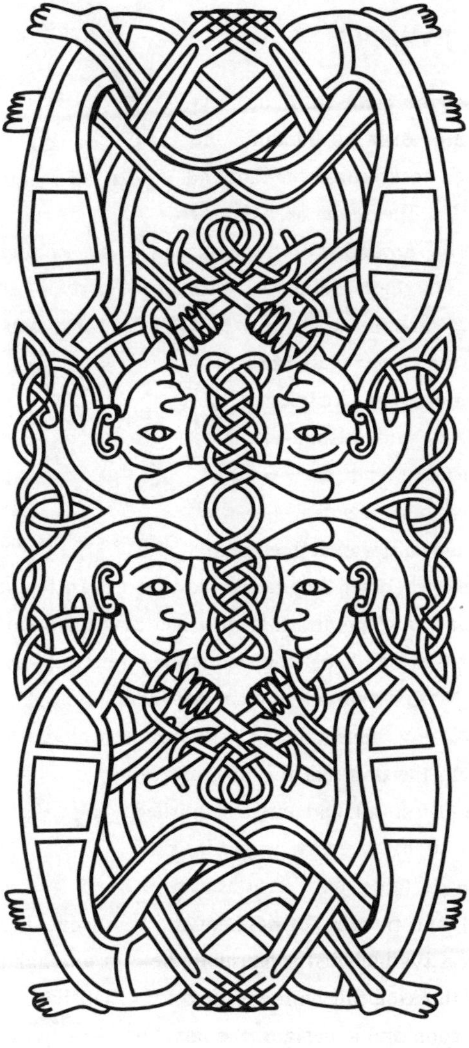

Book of kells

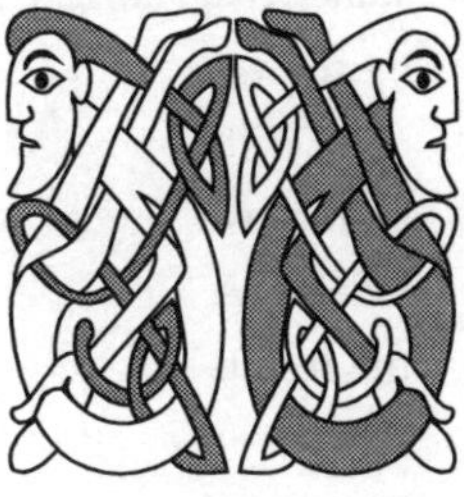

Book of kells

the Pictish Symbols

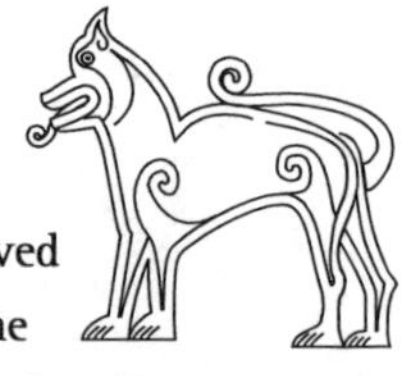

Papil, Shetland

All the images in this section come from the carved stones of the Picts on the east coast of Scotland. They have been dated to around the 6th century AD, and as such they coincide with the arrival of Christianity in the area. Many of these symbols are also found on the carved slab crosses, so there was obviously no religious objection to their use. Their symbolism may have come from Pagan times, but they were seen to symbolize Christian virtues as well.

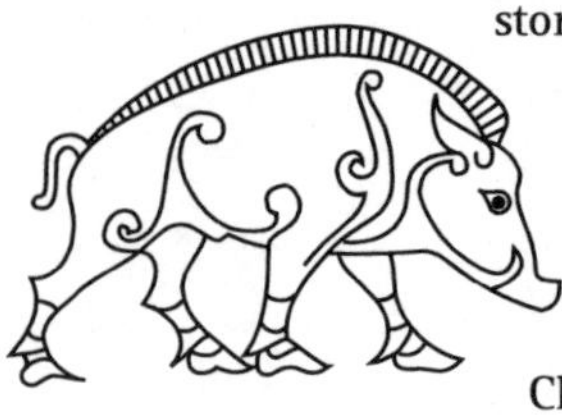

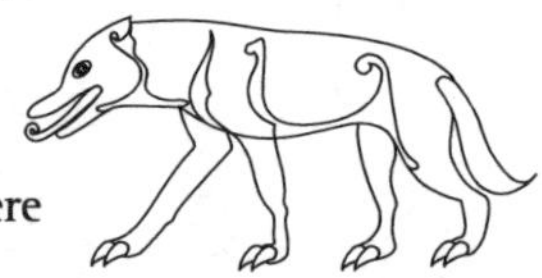

Ardross, Scotland

The fact that the symbols are well defined and already standard images (wherever they occur they are drawn in the same way) implies that they had developed earlier and that the slab stones were only the first permanent record of them.

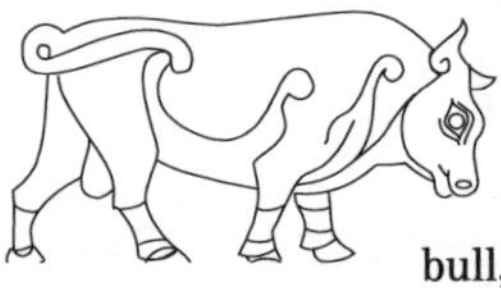

Various animals, such as the boar, the bull, the dog and the fish, are to be seen all over the area. These all had well established meanings. The boar stood for strength in battle, the bull for fertility and wealth (cows were used as currency among the Celts), and the dog for devotion and duty. The fish was a symbol of wisdom after the famous Celtic salmon. Horses' heads are a common image, but there seems to be little or no standardization in their design, possibly because they are pictures of particular horses and as such

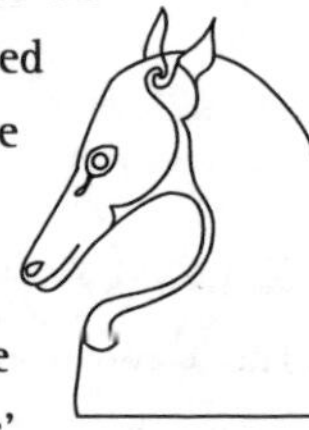

Ardross, Scotland

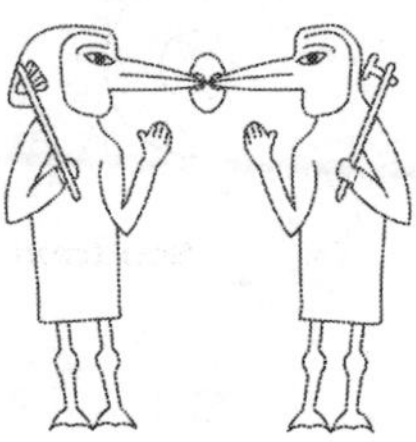

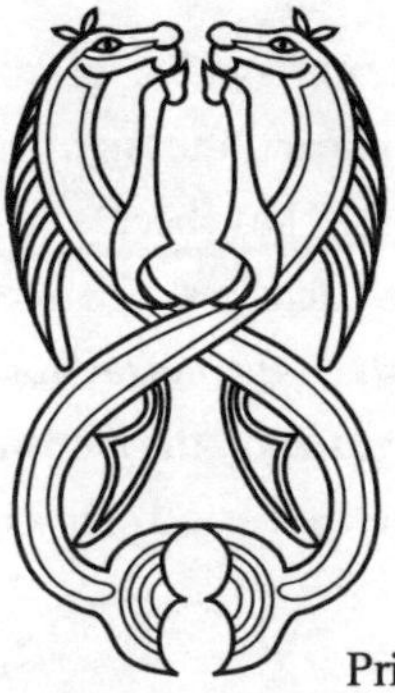

rely on the artist drawing realistically.

In contrast to the realism of the symbolic animals various fantastic creatures are also carved on the stones. The most outlandish are the pair of bird-headed people from Papil, Shetland, who appear more Egyptian than Celtic. However, they are not the only ones. A bird-headed person is carved on a slab stone at Rossie Priory, Scotland, with bizarre creatures, including two llama-like animals with human heads and snake-head tails. There are at least two versions of a seahorse design. The significance of all these creatures is lost to us now.

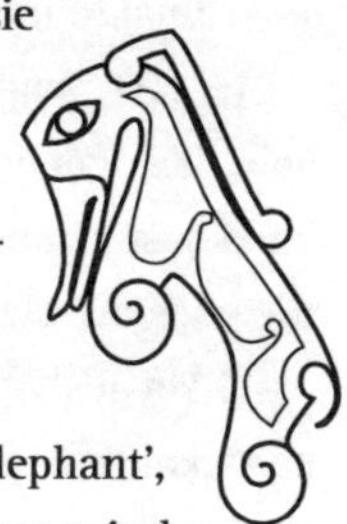

The most common fantastic creature was the 'elephant', always standing on its rear spiral legs with a trunk or duck's beak. No one has yet come up with a plausible interpretation of this symbol, but it must have had a meaning to have been so widely and exactly copied. The topknot is closer to the early Celtic and Scandinavian styles that to that of locally made illuminated manuscripts.

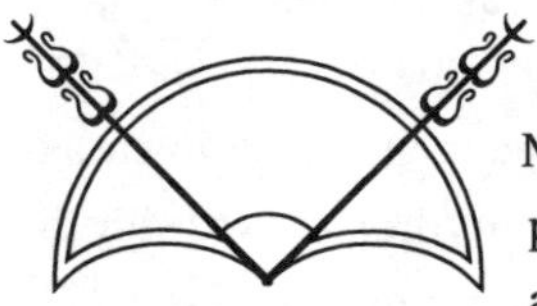

Aberlemno, Scotland

The next group is the purely graphical symbols. The 'V-rod' and the 'Z-rod' are always drawn as on the left. The semi-circle in the V-rod symbol is often filled with spiral or key pattern designs. The Z-rod is rarely as basic as that shown here; the circles tend to be filled with spiral and knotwork patterns, with all manner of fine decoration that has been lost to us over the last thousand years.

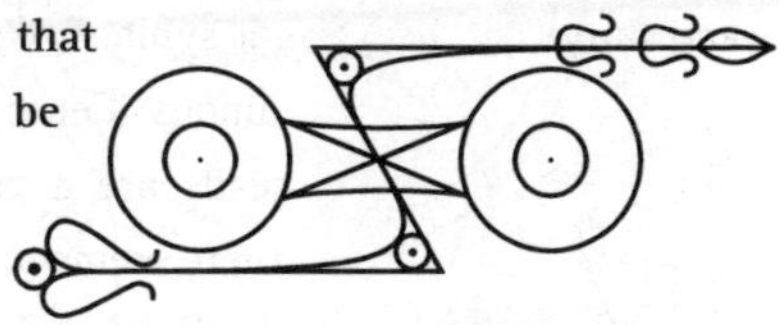

Aberlemno, Scotland

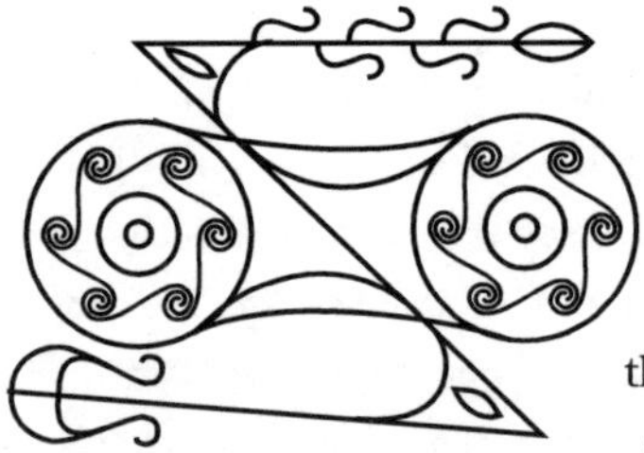

Aberlemno, Scotland

The most common symbol of all must be the mirror, the significance of which has been discussed already. Here we can see the similarity between the mirror and another symbol found on the Pictish stones, apparently a basic solar or solar temple image but obviously not a mirror.

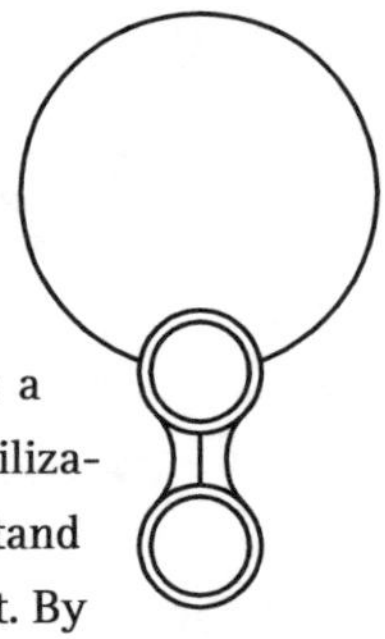

The last image is possibly the least understandable. It is generally described as a tuning fork but looks just as much like a broken sword – though as the ends are clean it is unlikely to be that.

Which just goes to show that although we have a remarkably large collection of images from this civilization that lasted for around two millennia, we understand very little about the people and the way they thought. By learning and practising their art we can hope to get closer to an age before the coming of the linear, urban culture that arrived with the Romans and is still with us today.

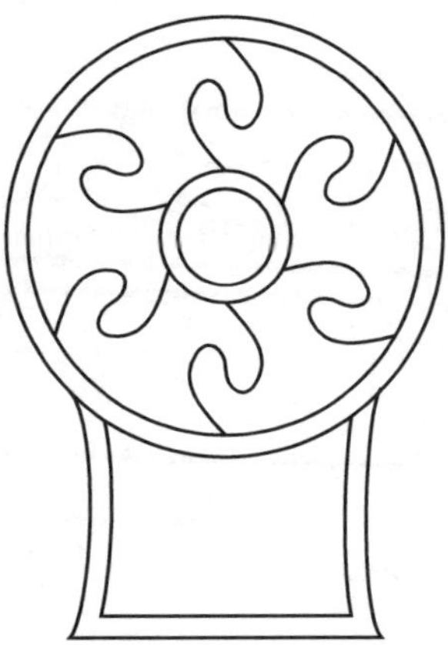

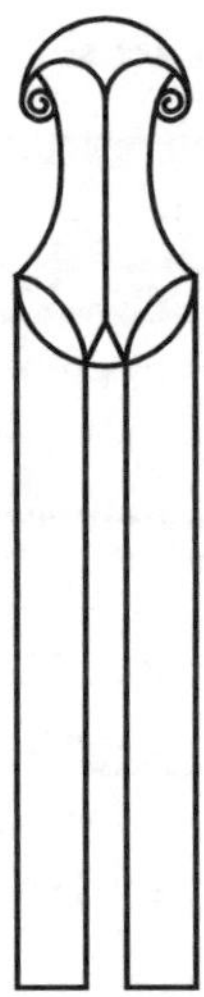

celtic
BODY PAINTING

IMPORTANT NOTE

BODY PAINT IS FOR EXTERNAL USE ONLY

WARNING

Avoid any contact with the eyes. However, if you do get any of the substances contained in this pack in the eyes do not rub them, wash immediately with cold water, or rinse with an eye bath. If symptoms persist, then consult your doctor immediately.

Test to ensure you are not allergic to the body paint. Place a drop of paint on the back of your hand and wait a few minutes. Wipe off the paint. If there is any sign of irritation then do not proceed with the application

Body paint does leave stains, so protect your work area with sheets or newspapers, cover your clothes and keep away from upholstery.

INSTRUCTIONS FOR BODY PAINT APPLICATION

(*Before you start, we recommend that you read the full instructions on pages 21 to 27 of the book included in this kit – the chapter entitled* Creating Your Own Body Art)

If you are using the transfer template included in this kit, select your required design, cut roughly around the edge and place it in position on an area of skin dampened with water. Press down on the transfer for several seconds with some damp cotton wool until the image is flat. Lift off and you will be left with an impression of the design on your skin. If necessary, smooth over with the cotton wool to ensure adhesion. Paint over this with the body paints included in this kit.